SAINT ROMANOS THE MELODIST

Hymns of Repentance

T0366616

ST VLADIMIR'S SEMINARY PRESS
Popular Patristics Series
Number 61

The Popular Patristics Series published by St Vladimir's Seminary Press provides readable and accurate translations of a wide range of early Christian literature to a wide audience—students of Christian history to lay Christians reading for spiritual benefit. Recognized scholars in their fields provide short but comprehensive and clear introductions to the material. The texts include classics of Christian literature, thematic volumes, collections of homilies, letters on spiritual counsel, and poetical works from a variety of geographical contexts and historical backgrounds. The mission of the series is to mine the riches of the early Church and to make these treasures available to all.

Series Editor
BOGDAN BUCUR

Associate Editor
IGNATIUS GREEN

* * *

Series Editor
1999–2020
JOHN BEHR

SAINT ROMANOS THE MELODIST

*H*ymns of *R*epentance

Introduction, Translation, and Notes by
ANDREW MELLAS

ST VLADIMIR'S SEMINARY PRESS

YONKERS, NEW YORK

Library of Congress Control Number: 2020930867

COPYRIGHT © 2020 BY
ST VLADIMIR'S SEMINARY PRESS
575 Scarsdale Road, Yonkers, NY 10707
1-800-204-2665
www.svspress.com

ISBN 978–088141–657–2 (paper)
ISBN 978–088141–658–9 (kindle)
ISSN 1555–5755

PRINTED IN THE UNITED STATES OF AMERICA

To Romanos

Contents

Introduction

Despite the fame that St Romanos the Melodist enjoyed in Byzantium and beyond, we know precious little about his life.[1] The short narrative of his career emerges centuries after his lifetime (c. 490–560) in manuscripts such as the *Menologion of Basil II*:

> The venerable Romanos was from Syria and became a deacon of the holy church of Berytos. Arriving in Constantinople in the reign of the emperor Anastasios, he went and settled in the church of the most holy Theotokos in the *ta Kyrou* district, where he received the gift of the *kontakia*. In piety he would celebrate and pass the night, praying during the vigil at Blachernae, before returning to *ta Kyrou*. On one of these nights, the most holy Theotokos appeared to him while he was asleep and gave him a paper scroll and said, "Take this paper and eat it." It seems that the saint opened his mouth and swallowed the paper. Now it was the festival of Christ's Nativity. And, immediately awakening from his sleep, he was astonished and glorified God. Thereupon he mounted the ambo and began to chant, "Today the Virgin gives birth to him who is above all being." He also composed nearly one thousand *kontakia* for other festivals before departing for the Lord.[2]

[1] For an analysis of the biographical sources available on Romanos, see José Grosdidier de Matons, *Romanos le Mélode et les origines de la poésie religieuse à Byzance* (Paris: Beauchesne, 1977), 159–98.

[2] For the Greek text, see Grosdidier de Matons, *Romanos le Mélode*, 161–62. I have based my translation into English on translations by Derek Krueger and the late Archimandrite Ephrem Lash. See Derek Krueger, *Writing and Holiness: The Practice of Authorship in the Early Christian East* (Philadelphia: University of Pennsylvania Press, 2004), 189; Lash, ed. *On the Life of Christ: Chanted Sermons by the Great Sixth-Century Poet and Singer St. Romanos* (Lanham, MD: AltaMira Press, 1998), xxvii.

While the text suggests Romanos wrote one thousand hymns, only 89 are attributed to him in extant manuscripts, of which almost 60 are considered genuine.[3] Most notable is the account of Romanos' miraculous birth as a hymnographer, which sees the Theotokos act as a kind of Byzantine Muse who inspires the composition and performance of his most famous hymn, *On the Nativity*.[4]

The *Menologion of Basil II* confirms that Romanos' literary output took place in Constantinople during the reign of Emperor Justinian, which is evident from Romanos' own hymns. One of Romanos' hymns, *On Earthquakes and Fires*, sings the praises of Justinian and alludes to the reconstruction of Hagia Sophia.[5] Justinian's reign was an age of political and cultural transformation.[6] Alongside the military, legal, and architectural accomplishments of Justinian, a prolific literary culture began to flourish.[7] Romanos played a pivotal role in this emerging milieu, straddling the worlds of antiquity and Byzantium. His poetry represents a unique fusion of classical rhetoric inherited from the Greek world of antiquity, the fourth-century Syriac poetry of St Ephrem, and the Christian discourse of the Cappadocian Fathers.

[3]Romanos the Melodist, *Sancti Romani Melodi Cantica: Cantica Genuina*, ed. Paul Maas and C. A. Trypanis (Oxford: Clarendon Press, 1963). José Grosdidier de Matons believes a few of the kontakia, which Maas and Trypanis think are dubious, to be genuine. See Romanos le Mélode, *Hymnes*, ed. José Grosdidier de Matons, 5 vols., Sources Chrétiennes 99, 110, 114, 128, 283 (Paris: Éditions du Cerf, 1964–1981).

[4]Romanos' ingestion of the scroll echoes the biblical accounts of the prophet Ezekiel (Ezek 3.1–3) and John the Evangelist (Rev 10.8–9).

[5]Romanos le Mélode, *Hymnes. Tome V: Nouveau Testament et Hymnes de Circonstance*, ed. Grosdidier de Matons. SC 283 (Paris: Éditions du Cerf, 1981), 470–99. See also Eva Catafygiotu Topping, "On Earthquakes and Fires: Romanos' Encomium to Justinian," *Byzantinische Zeitschrifte* 71.1 (1978): 22–35.

[6]Michael Maas, "Roman Questions, Byzantine Answers: Contours of the Age of Justinian," in *The Cambridge Companion to the Age of Justinian*, ed. Michael Maas (Cambridge: Cambridge University Press, 2005), 3–27.

[7]See Louth, "Justinian and his Legacy," in *The Cambridge History of the Byzantine Empire c. 500–1492*, ed. Jonathan Shepard (Cambridge: Cambridge University Press, 2008), 99–129; Claudia Rapp, "Literary Culture under Justinian," in *The Cambridge Companion to the Age of Justinian*, 376–400.

The kontakion and its liturgical context

The history of Byzantine hymnography has occasionally been portrayed as a tale of two genres: *kontakion* and *kanōn*.[8] Despite mistaken perceptions that the "*kanon* replaced the *kontakion* toward the end of the seventh century,"[9] the story is not so simple. After Romanos' lifetime, the kontakion was neither neglected as a liturgical genre nor did it fall into obscurity.[10] Indeed, "far from falling into disuse from the eighth century onwards," the kontakion "continued to flourish until the twelfth century."[11] Rather than the kanon supplanting the kontakion in the office of matins, the liturgical place of the kontakion was to be found elsewhere.[12]

The elements of a kontakion included at least one prelude introducing the polystrophic poem, a series of metrically identical strophes developing the narrative, and a refrain acting as a unifying thread for all the strophes.[13] Romanos also weaves an acrostic as a kind of poetic signature—for example, "by the humble Romanos"—through the strophes, which is evidence that he wrote the hymns.[14] Rhythmically, the kontakion is based on stress accent rather than the quantitative metres of classical Greek that St Gregory

[8]Egon Wellesz, *A History of Byzantine Music and Hymnography* (Oxford: Clarendon Press, 1961), 179–239. A *kanon* is a set of eight or nine odes for matins.

[9]Leena Mari Peltomaa, "Hymnography, Byzantine," in *The Encyclopedia of Ancient History,* ed. Roger S. Bagnall, et al. (Malden: Wiley-Blackwell 2013), 3363.

[10]Grosdidier de Matons, "Liturgie et Hymnographie: Kontakion et Canon," *Dumbarton Oaks Papers* 34/35 (1980–81): 31–43.

[11]Louth, "Christian Hymnography from Romanos the Melodist to John Damascene," *Journal of Early Christian Studies* 57 (2005): 199. See also Mary B. Cunningham, "The Reception of Romanos in Middle Byzantine Homiletics and Hymnography," *Dumbarton Oaks Papers* 62 (2008): 251–60.

[12]Alexander Lingas, "The Liturgical Place of the Kontakion in Constantinople," in *Liturgy, Architecture and Art of the Byzantine World: Papers of the XVIII International Byzantine Congress* (*Moscow, 8–15 August 1991) and Other Essays Dedicated to the Memory of Fr. John Meyendorff,* ed. C. C. Akentiev (St Petersburg: Vizantinorossika, 1995), 50–57.

[13]Grosdidier de Matons, *Romanos le Mélode,* 37–48.

[14]Interestingly, Romanos did not refer to his hymns as kontakia but as hymns, poems and prayers.

the Theologian's poetry favored.[15] Although Romanos' kontakia display these formal elements, their dramatic meditation on scriptural characters' personal thoughts and sensory perceptions set them apart.[16]

The kontakion was an integral part of the cathedral rite in Constantinople until the Fourth Crusade in 1204.[17] It formed part of the night vigil (παννυχίς, *pannychis*), which was celebrated in anticipation of major feasts in the liturgical calendar.[18] Romanos himself describes this ritual in his hymn *On the Man Possessed with Demons*:

> The people of Christ, faithful in their love,
> have gathered to keep vigil with psalms and odes;
> unceasingly they sing hymns to God.
> Now that the Psalms of David have been sung,
> and we were gladdened by the well-ordered
>   reading of Scripture,
> let us again raise a hymn to Christ and denounce
>   the enemies.[19]

In addition to referring to the night vigil, these lines evoke a vivid image of how the faithful experienced this liturgical gathering and

[15]See, for example, *Gregory of Nazianzus: Autobiographical Poems*, Carolinne White, trans. (Cambridge: Cambridge University Press, 1996).

[16]See Georgia Frank, "Dialogue and Deliberation: The Sensory Self in the Hymns of Romanos the Melodist," in *Religion and the Self in Antiquity*, ed. David Brakke, M. L. Satlow, and S. Wetzman (Indianapolis: Bloomington, 2005), 163–79; Derek Krueger, "Romanos the Melodist and the Early Christian Self," in *Proceedings of the 21st International Congress of Byzantine Studies: London, 21–26 August 2006*, ed. Elizabeth Jeffreys (Aldershot: Ashgate, 2006), 255–74.

[17]Lingas, "The Liturgical Place of the Kontakion," 53. For further background on this ritual, see Miguel Arranz, "N. D. Uspensky: The Office of the All-night Vigil in the Greek Church and in the Russian Church," *St Vladimir's Theological Quarterly* 24 (1980): 169–74.

[18]Frank, "Romanos and the Night Vigil," 63.

[19]For the Greek text, see Romanos le Mélode, *Hymnes. Tome III: Nouveau Testament*, ed. Grosdidier de Matons, SC 114 (Paris: Éditions du Cerf, 1965), 54, 56. The English translation is my own.

the performance of Romanos' hymns. Scriptural meditation was combined with poetry and melody—psalmody and kontakion. The text also alludes to the faithful partaking in the singing of hymns, explicitly inviting them to do so through the use of verbs in the hortatory voice—"let us raise a hymn (ἀνυμνήσωμεν)" and "let us denounce (στηλιτεύσωμεν)".

The *Miracles of St Artemios* also mentions the performance of Romanos' kontakia during the night vigil. According to this text, Romanos' kontakia were sung a century after his death as part of the night vigil at the church of St John the Baptist in the Constantinopolitan quarter of Oxeia, which was where the relic of St Artemios was to be found.[20] Miracle 18, which recounts a burglary, is particularly insightful:

> There was a certain man who from a tender age used to attend the all-night vigil of the Forerunner and who sang the hymns of humble Romanos among the saints right up to the present day. In the time of the reign of Emperor Herakleios, this man was burglarized as the birthday of the holy Forerunner was dawning.[21]

What is remarkable in the account of this miracle is that a member of a lay congregation who was not the cantor participated in the singing of Romanos' kontakia. Moreover, the performance of Romanos' hymns continued for several centuries after his death and not necessarily in monastic settings, but at liturgical events open to the wider Constantinopolitan community.[22]

[20]*The Miracles of St. Artemios: A Collection of Miracle Stories by an Anonymous Author of Seventh-Century Byzantium*, Virgil S. Crisafulli and John W. Nesbitt, eds. (Leiden: Brill, 1997), 174–75.
[21]Ibid., 114–15.
[22]Frank, "Romanos and the Night Vigil," 66; Lingas, "The Liturgical Place of the Kontakion," 53.

Manuscripts, Editions, and Translations

Kontakia are found in two manuscript traditions that emerged between the tenth and thirteenth centuries in Byzantium—the *Kontakarion* (pl. *Kontakaria*) and the *Psaltikon* (pl. *Psaltika*). The former generally preserved the text of the hymns for the liturgical calendar.[23] The latter contained musical notation for liturgical use by the soloist and originated in the cathedral rite of Constantinople.[24] The modern critical editions of Romanos' kontakia by the Oxford editors, Maas and Trypanis, and by the French scholar, Grosdidier de Matons, rely on these manuscript traditions. While this edition of Romanos' Lenten hymns has consulted these critical editions, it has also examined the tenth-century Patmos *Kontakarion*, which consists of two codices: Patmos 212 and 213.[25]

The Greek text of the Romanos' hymns in this edition is based on the work of Maas, Trypanis, and Grosdidier de Matons. However, it also closely reflects the text in the Patmos *Kontakarion*, with few variations. In order to highlight the refrain, which in the manuscript is capitalized, this edition places the words of the refrain in boldface type.

While the Greek text in this edition is spaced in such a way that it suggests the metrical scheme of each hymn, for a comprehensive analysis of these schemes, the reader is encouraged to consult the critical editions of Romanos' hymns.

[23]Grosdidier de Matons, *Romanos le Mélode*, 67–118. However, there are some *Kontakaria* that also contain musical notation.

[24]Christian Troelsgård, *Byzantine Neumes: A New Introduction to the Middle Byzantine Notation* (Copenhagen: Museum Tusculanum Press, 2011), 85. To confuse matters, some *Psaltika* are referred to as *Kontakaria*. See for example the Florentine *Psaltikon* that was copied at the monastery of Grottaferrata during the thirteenth century in Carsten Høeg, *Contacarium Ashburnhamense: Codex Bibl. Laurentianae Ashburnhamensis 64 phototypice depictus*, MMB Série Principale 4 (Copenhagen: Ejnar Munksgaard, 1956).

[25]The first codex is for the cycle of fixed feasts and the second codex is for the moveable cycle. Although I have examined both, Patmos 213 contains the hymns edited and translated in the present volume. Patmos 213 begins with Meatfare Sunday and ends with the Tuesday of Pentecost.

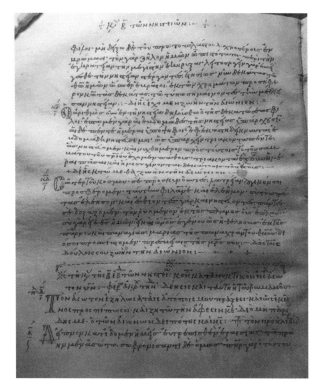

Figure 1: Patmos 213, folio 21v, which shows the end of Romanos' hymn *On Fasting* and the beginning of his hymn *On the Prodigal Son*. Permission granted by the Library of the Monastery of St John the Theologian (Patmos, Greece).

An English translation of all the kontakia attributed to Romanos—genuine and dubious—is yet to be released. Translations by Marjorie Carpenter, Robert Schork, and the late Archimandrite Ephrem Lash are available, though they are often difficult to find.[26]

[26]Lash, *On the Life of Christ*; Romanos the Melodist, *Sacred Song from the Byzantine Pulpit: Romanos the Melodist*, trans. R. J. Schork (Gainesville: University Press of Florida, 1995); *Kontakia of Romanos, Byzantine Melodist*, 2 vols., trans. Marjorie Carpenter (Columbia: University of Missouri Press, 1970–73).

While all translations from the Greek text of Romanos' hymns in this edition are my own, I have consulted translations by the aforementioned authors. I am particularly indebted to Lash's translations. I would also like to acknowledge the helpful reflections of Fr John Behr, Fr Ignatius Green, Dr John A. L. Lee, and Andrew Psarommatis on some of my initial translations of some difficult strophes from the hymns in this edition. As always, any shortcomings are my own.

Romanos' Lenten Hymns

In the Byzantine liturgical calendar, Great Lent was preceded by three preparatory Sundays and it culminated in Holy Week.[27] Out of the 59 genuine kontakia in the manuscript tradition, almost half (27) were sung during this liturgical cycle. Within the confines of this edition, it is not possible to translate all of these hymns, even if the hymns for the preparatory Sundays and Holy Week were excluded. Therefore, I have chosen seven hymns by Romanos that were sung during the course of Great Lent and which share a common theme: repentance.

Although the manuscript tradition usually assigns each kontakion to a particular day in the liturgical calendar, this does not necessarily reflect when each hymn was sung in sixth-century Constantinople. I recognize that our knowledge of liturgical practice and the lectionary in the sixth century is scant, owing to the fact that no liturgical books relating to Constantinopolitan worship survive from that century. While the manuscript tradition probably reflects the liturgical practices of prior centuries, I acknowledge that there remains uncertainty in relation to Romanos' time. The prehistory of the Byzantine liturgical calendar is still being written. Nevertheless, as a liturgical phenomenon that extended beyond the lifetime of the

[27]Indeed, the Byzantine hymnal for this period, the *Triodion*, begins with these preparatory Sundays (commemorating the prodigal son, the Last Judgment, and the exile of Adam and Eve from Eden) and ends on Holy Saturday. For an overview of this liturgical cycle in Byzantium, including the preparatory period and Holy Week, see Archbishop Job Getcha's *The Typikon Decoded: An Explanation of Byzantine Liturgical Practice* (Yonkers, NY: St Vladimir's Seminary Press, 2012), 141–232

hymnographer, the performance of Romanos' hymns during sacred rituals is something that generations of faithful in Constantinople would experience for centuries after his death.

I have also focused on hymns that are portrayed as arousing compunction.[28] Compunction colors the entire Lenten cycle and its hymnography in the *Triodion*.[29] The word compunction today conveys a sense of remorse but usually in a weakened sense.[30] However, in Late Antiquity and Byzantium, the feeling of compunction intertwined with the experience of paradisal nostalgia and an outpouring of tears. Compunction was also linked with repentance, which emerges as a leitmotif of Scripture, especially in Luke-Acts,[31] and late antique Christian discourse.[32] Unlike modern audiences, which have inherited "a somewhat distorted and incomplete view of repentance in late antiquity" as inextricably

---

[28]Indeed, several of Romanos' hymns are entitled "a *kontakion* of compunction" (κοντάκιον κατανυκτικόν) in the manuscript tradition. On the genre of compunctious literature in Byzantium, see Antonia Giannouli, "Catanyctic Religious Poetry: A Survey" in *Theologica Minora: The Minor Genres of Byzantine Theological Literature*, ed. Antonio Rigo, Pavel Ermilov, and Michele Trizio (Turnhout: Brepols, 2013), 86–109.

[29]In Byzantium, the *Triodion* was the liturgical book that contained hymns for the six weeks of Great Lent, a number of preparatory Sundays and feasts that preceded Great Lent, and Holy Week. The liturgical reforms of the Monastery of Saint John the Forerunner at Stoudios in Constantinople in the early ninth century were a watershed in the historical development of the *Triodion*. St Theodore the Stoudite (759–826), his brother St Joseph the Stoudite (762–832), and their successors collected, composed, and edited hymns written by various hymnographers since the fifth century, from Jerusalem, Constantinople, and other parts of the Byzantine Empire.

[30]Κατάνυξις is the Greek word for compunction in Byzantium. See G. W. H. Lampe, *Patristic Greek Lexicon* (Oxford: Clarendon Press, 1961), 713. The Greek word is not found in any writings from classical antiquity but makes its first appearance in the Septuagint.

[31]See Guy D. Nave, Jr., *The Role and Function of Repentance in Luke-Acts* (Leiden: Brill, 2002).

[32]For an introduction to the significance of repentance for Eastern Christendom and how the early church fathers interpreted the scriptural meaning of repentance, see Kallistos Ware, "The Orthodox Experience of Repentance," *Sobornost* 2 (1980): 18–28. For notions of repentance in monastic literature, see Brouria Bitton-Ash-kelony, "Penitence in Late Antique Monastic Literature," in *Transformations of the Inner Self in Ancient Religions,* ed. Jan Assmann and Guy G. Stroumsa (Leiden: Brill, 1999), 179–94.

connected with ecclesiastical institutions of penitence, repentance's existential significance for Christianity went beyond penitential rites, embracing the totality of Christian life.[33] Romanos' kontakia enacted this inclusive conception of repentance through narratives and songs that illuminated the relationships between repentance, compunction, and tears.

Although several of Romanos' hymns present a biblical figure as an exemplar of compunction and repentance, two of his kontakia are explicitly concerned with the overarching significance of this cata-logue of repentant sinners: *On the Repentance of the Ninevites* and *A Prayer*.[34] They are strategically placed at the beginning and near the end of the Lenten liturgical cycle as touchstones of repentance. *On the Repentance of the Ninevites* presents the narrative of the remorse-ful Ninevites as an image and song of collective repentance and *A Prayer* recapitulates various Lenten themes, such as eschatology and biblical exemplars of fallenness, compunction, and repentance, in a personal plea to God for salvation.

The performance of Romanos' hymn *On the Repentance of the Ninevites* took place during the Wednesday of the first week of the Lenten fast. This kontakion was sung only a few days after Cheese-Fare Sunday—the Sunday that enacted the exile of Adam and Eve from Eden.[35] This Sunday encapsulates the climate of paradisal nos-talgia and the sense of alienation from the divine that characterize the Byzantine journey of Lent. One of the hymns that is found in the

[33] Alexis Torrance, *Repentance in Late Antiquity. Eastern Asceticism and the Framing of the Christian Life* (Oxford: Oxford University Press, 2012), 9.

[34] *On the Repentance of the Ninevites* is a "compunctious kontakion" that was sung on the Wednesday of the first week of the Lenten fast. *A Prayer* is a "compunctious kontakion" that was chanted during the Wednesday of the fifth week of the Lenten fast.

[35] According to the fourteenth-century Byzantine historian, Nikephoros Kallis-tos Xanthopoulos, commemorating the exile of Adam and Eve from Eden on Cheese-Fare Sunday (the last Sunday of the pre-Lenten period) was an ancient practice—see Getcha, *The Typikon Decoded*, 160–61. Hymns narrating this biblical event can be found in three of the earliest manuscripts of the *Triodion*: Sinai Graecus 734–735, fols. 45r–49r, Vaticanus Graecus 771, fols. 30r–32r, and Grottaferrata Δβ I, fols. 28r–30v.

Triodion for this day dramatizes Adam's lament at being banished from the "bliss of Paradise" in the form of a soliloquy, during which he exclaims on three occasions: "Woe is me!"[36] The anonymous composition *On the Lament of Adam*[37] invites the faithful to sing the words of Adam in the refrain of the hymns as if they were the cry of all Christians: "O Merciful One, have mercy on the one who has fallen."[38]

According to the *Prophetologion*, the Old Testament lectionary of Constantinople,[39] the worshipping faithful heard passages from Genesis during Lenten vespers, beginning on the first Monday of Lent and ending on Palm Sunday.[40] The narrative of the exile of Adam and Eve was read during vespers on Friday of the first week of Lent.[41] Therefore, the refrain of *On the Lament of Adam* subtly echoed the metanarrative of repentance and salvation that recurs throughout Romanos' kontakia, highlighting the moment of epiphany when the journey of homecoming begins.

[36]Kallistos Ware and Mother Mary, *The Lenten Triodion* (Boston: Faber, 1978), 178. This hymn is found in two of the earliest manuscripts of the *Triodion*: Sinai Graecus 734–735, fol. 46r, and Grottaferrata Δβ I, fol. 28v.

[37]For the Greek text of this late fifth-century, early sixth-century hymn, see Paul Maas, *Frühbyzantinische Kirchenpoesie: I. Anonyme Hymnen des V–VI Jahrhunderts* (Berlin: De Gruyter, 1931), 16–20.

[38]For an exploration of how the voice of Adam and the voice of the Christian were fused in the performance of Byzantine hymns such as *On the Lament of Adam*, see Derek Krueger, *Liturgical Subjects: Christian Ritual, Biblical Narrative, and the Formation of Self in Byzantium* (Philadelphia: University of Pennsylvania Press, 2014), 186–91.

[39]*Prophetologium*, Carsten Høeg, Günther Zuntz, and Gundrun Engberg, eds. (Copenhagen: Ejnar Munksgaard, 1939–81).

[40]The *Prophetologion* itself emerged in the eighth century but may have reflected earlier lectionary practices in Constantinople that evolved before the sixth century. See Sysse Gundrun Engberg, "The *Prophetologion* and the Triple-Lection Theory—the Genesis of a Liturgical Book," *Bollettino della Badia Greca di Grottaferrata*, no. 3 (2006): 67–91; James Miller, "The Prophetologion: The Old Testament of Byzantine Christianity?" in *The Old Testament in Byzantium*, ed. Paul Magdalino and Robert Nelson (Washington, DC: Dumbarton Oaks, 2010), 55–76.

[41]See the readings for the first and second weeks of Lent in volume one (fasciculus secundus, 1940) of Høeg, Zuntz, and Engberg, *Prophetologium*, 150–54.

Although the narrative structure of Romanos' *On the Repentance of the Ninevites* was the Old Testament story of how the Ninevites' city was delivered from impending doom, its broader liturgical and ascetic context framed the meaning of its meditation on repentance. Indeed, a week after this kontakion was performed, on Wednesday of the second week of Lent, Romanos' hymn *On Fasting* explored the significance of abstinence, which is only briefly mentioned in *On the Repentance of the Ninevites*. *On Fasting* portrayed fasting as "the holy mother of sound judgment" that "overflows with philosophy" and "gains us Paradise" which Adam lost: "by dishonoring the dignity of fasting he brought in death."[42]

Romanos' hymn *On the Repentance of the Ninevites* juxtaposes the biblical story from a bygone era with his contemporary reality of the people of Constantinople in the prelude of the kontakion,[43] inviting all to the "infirmary of repentance" in the first strophe. The medical imagery presents sin as a sickness of the soul and repentance as its remedy. In inviting the faithful to the infirmary of spiritual healing, Romanos momentarily strays from his story. He repeatedly invokes the hortatory voice and weaves the story of the Ninevites together with other stories of repentance from the Old and New Testaments. The unifying threads in these narratives of repentance are tears and compunction. Indeed, "tears are cherished, beloved, and desired by the deliverer,"[44] they "washed away the filth of the city,"[45] and they can paradoxically overcome the omnipotence of God.

Romanos does not portray tears of compunction as incorporeal; he suggests their source—the innermost depths of the human person—differs from that of other tears, such as tears of sorrow or tears of pain. *On the Repentance of the Ninevites* depicts compunction and tears as having the power to purify a city and to summon God's mercy. In presenting repentance as an infirmary, the hymn's imagery

---

[42]Strophe 4.
[43]"Lord, show compassion even now on your people and your city."
[44]Strophe 2.
[45]Strophe 5.

echoes St Gregory of Nyssa's portrayal of tears as "blood from the wounds of the soul"[46] leading to repentance.[47]

Encouraging the faithful to weep from their hearts like the Ninevites of old, Romanos' hymn *On the Repentance of the Ninevites* enacts the collective feeling and cosmic implications of a city's compunction and repentance. Although the final strophe reverts to the first-person singular, ending with a personal prayer for repentance, the previous strophes dramatize the salvation of the Ninevites and God's compassion in the face of their compunction. The congregation's singing of the refrain—"he accepts our repentance"—and its variations, their familiarity with the kontakion and its story, which was sung every year in the first week of Lent, and their experience of the *pannychis*, became their litugical scripts through which they besought the tears of compunction that saved the Ninevites.

This theme is more pronounced in Romanos' *A Prayer*, which four weeks later would invite the faithful to cry out and ask God for tears that purify the soul through compunction. To underscore why this catharsis of tears is vital, Romanos invoked the nuptial metaphor of the soul's union with the Creator, which echoed the allegorical interpretation of the Song of Songs that Origen and Gregory of Nyssa had propounded. The context for this personal plea is an intricate image presented by the prelude of the kontakion in the form of a dialogue between self and soul. Romanos encourages the faithful to become introspective and remember events from the past and the future as they partake in the affective mysticism of hymnody. The refrain of *A Prayer* would have become the entreaty of the faithful as the kontakion was sung and it echoed the Ninevites' song of repentance, which the congregation sang on their behalf.

[46]Gregory of Nyssa, *Funeral Oration on the Empress Flacilla* in PG 46:880C and *Gregorii Nysseni Opera* IX, ed. Andreas Spira (Leiden: Brill, 1967), 477.
[47]It also points to what the word *compunction* originally signified. Before Christianity transposed its meaning, κατάνυξις denoted physical pain rather than a metaphorical piercing of the heart. See Michael S. Driscoll, "Compunction," in *Catholic Dictionary of Spirituality*, ed. Michael Downey (Collegeville, MN: Liturgical Press, 1995), 193.

As the Byzantine faithful journeyed through Great Lent and Holy Week, Romanos' hymns presented them with biblical exemplars of compunction, retelling scriptural stories and welcoming them to enter into these narratives. The parable of the prodigal son and other narratives that juxtaposed biblical heroes with counter-ideals such as the foolish virgins and Judas, were enriched with melody and dramatic dialogue as the hymnographer explored the emotions of his protagonists and dramatised their repentance.

The first hymn that presented the faithful with a biblical exemplar of compunction during the Lenten cycle was *On the Prodigal*.[48] Although it is unclear from the manuscript tradition whether Romanos' *On the Prodigal* was performed on the Second Sunday of Lent or on the first of the three preparatory Sundays preceding Lent (before the fourteenth century in Constantinople the Second Sunday of Lent had no particular theme).[49] Moreover, the *Typikon of the Great Church* does not assign Luke 15.11–32 (the parable of the prodigal son) as the gospel reading for that Sunday.[50] Instead, this biblical passage is prescribed for the first of the three preparatory Sundays preceding Lent—"the Sunday before Meatfare Sunday."[51]

The two preludes in *On the Prodigal* open the hymn by asking the congregation to identify their "senseless deeds" with those of the prodigal son who befouled "the first garment of grace"—a baptismal image that is developed further in the fourth strophe—with "the stains of passions." As the prodigal son "came to himself"[52] and

---

[48]This is a "kontakion of compunction" about repentance and forgiveness that was chanted either during the Second Sunday of Lent—according to the Patmiacus 213 manuscript—or on the first of the three preparatory Sundays preceding Lent—according to the Athous Vatopedinus 1041 manuscript.

[49]Getcha, *The Typikon Decoded*, 189.

[50]Juan Mateos, *Le Typicon de la Grande Église: Tome II, Le Cycle des Fêtes Mobiles*. OCA 166 (Rome: Pontificum Institutum Orientalium Studiorum, 1963), 30. Instead, the passage from Mark 2.1–12 (the healing of the paralytic) is prescribed. It is only the Hagiopolite tradition and its lectionaries emerging from Jerusalem that assigns this passage to the Second Sunday of Lent. See Getcha, *The Typikon Decoded*, 146.

[51]Mateos, *Le Typicon: Tome II*, 2.

[52]Luke 15.17.

arose to return to his father's house, likewise the kontakion calls each of the faithful back to the "mystical table,"[53] which is an image of the Eucharist. Romanos presents the prodigal son as a paradigm of humanity who travels to a faraway land and—not unlike Adam— acknowledges his fallenness, feels compunction and nostalgia, and begins the journey home. It is through the prism of his repentance that Romanos invites the faithful to see and hear every other monologue and dialogue in the hymn, as well as the eucharistic and baptismal themes that emerge.

The hymn likens the robe that the prodigal son is given upon his repentance to "the first robe, which the baptismal font weaves for all."[54] This "first robe" symbolizes the ancient glory of Adam and Eve before they were given the "garments of skin"[55] and represents the common gift of all Christians who have been "baptized into Christ" and have "put on Christ."[56] Therefore in encouraging the faithful to imitate the prodigal son's repentance, Romanos unlocks the significance of his compunction for all Christians. And in dramatizing the father's compassion for his son with a monologue that does not appear in the Lukan narrative, the hymnographer demonstrates God's desire for all of his creation to be found worthy of forgiveness:

> I saw him and I cannot allow myself to overlook his nakedness;
>> I cannot bear to see my divine image like this.
> For the disgrace of my child is my shame;
> I will consider the glory of my child my own glory.[57]

Here Romanos begins to allude to the salvific acts of Christ—the crucifixion, descent into hades, and resurrection—the passion that

[53]Prelude 2.

[54]Strophe 4.

[55]Genesis 3.21. Indeed, as noted earlier, the worshipping faithful heard passages from Genesis during Lenten vespers, so the narrative of the exile from Eden was a recurring theme during Great Lent.

[56]Galatians 3.27.

[57]Strophe 5. The phrase "my divine image" is an allusion to Genesis 1.26.

will mark the climax of the Lenten journey. Although it is still the beginning of the Lenten season and these events have not yet come to pass, the ritual aesthetic of Byzantine hymns creates a rich dialectic between what has happened before and will occur again.

Romanos' exegesis of the fatted calf and the banquet, which mark the festivities for the prodigal's return, begins to collapse into the present liturgical moment events that took place long ago with what will be celebrated at the end of Great Lent and Holy Week. The human drama of the prodigal son's compunction and repentance unfolds amidst the divine drama of God's compassion, incarnation, and sacrifice:

> Drag in, sacrifice, the giver of life,
> who is sacrificed and not put to death,
> who gives life to those in hell,
> so that, as we eat, we may celebrate.[58]

The hymn's allusion to the Eucharist suggests that the celebration of the liturgy in Hagia Sophia and the other churches of Constantinople was imminent. The repentance of the prodigal climaxes not simply in a reconciliation with his father, but in the eucharistic celebration where all are given "the Lover of humankind" as "all-holy food."[59]

On the Prodigal ends with a prayer to the Logos of God to accept through compassion all those who like the prodigal son cry out with compunction. Once again Romanos brings other scriptural characters into his story, offering the figures of the publican and the harlot as paradigms of repentance. And, in an unexpected twist to the familiar biblical narrative, Romanos adds a new ending to the Lukan account. The prodigal son's elder brother, who in the gospel story refuses to enter the banquet and celebrate his younger brother's return, is persuaded by the love of his father to partake in the supper and sing with joy.[60]

[58]Strophe 8.
[59]Strophe 9.
[60]Strophe 21.

Romanos' hymn *On the Rich Man and Lazarus* was sung a few days before Holy Week on the Thursday of the sixth week of Lent. Romanos presents the faithful with a striking juxtaposition between the righteous Lazarus and the counter-ideal of the rich man by revealing their fate in the afterlife and amplifying the biblical narrative of Luke 16.19–31. Whereas the rich man was consigned to the fire of Gehenna, Christ escorted Lazarus to the bosom of Abraham. Once again, the purpose of this hymn is to invite the faithful to see the multitude of their own sins, but to call on the compassion and mercy of the Logos.

As is often the case in the hymns by Romanos, biblical protagonists who may be silent in Scripture (such as the harlot of Luke 7.36–50) are given a voice. In strophe 8, Lazarus, who does not utter a word in the Lukan narrative, says:

> "Long ago in times of old Job became poor, but remaining firm
>   under the blow,
> he was delivered from it.
> But I see death at hand before me,
> wherefore do not disregard me but receive my spirit, for I am
>   forsaken by all as a dead person,
> therefore, I am departing now and I will not be sad
> when I am dwelling in a tomb as in a house,
> as dust descending on the earth. But, my God, deliver me from
>   hades, as I cry out:
> *have mercy, O Lord.*"

Following this strophe, in a poignant and beautiful image, the angels suddenly come to Lazarus as friends who beguile him and suffer with him. In stark contrast, the rich man soon finds himself in hades, marvelling at the one whom he did not deem worthy of crumbs: "And how great a splendor and glory does he have, which I did not see on the earth?"[61] When the rich man calls out to Abraham and pleads for mercy, the reply of the patriarch is laced with

[61]Strophe 14.

a dose of compunction: "Behold you call me father, not perceiving my hospitality; otherwise, seeing Lazarus in poverty, you would not have overlooked him."[62] The dialogue between the two characters invites the faithful to "ponder the things of God" and not to "live in vain."[63]

Romanos' *On the Infernal Powers* and *On the Victory of the Cross* are hymns that touch upon the theme of eschatology.[64] Although the eschaton often denoted the last things—the end of the world and its final judgment by God—in Byzantine Christian thought, the eschaton was not simply a future occurrence but a liturgical reality experienced in the Eucharist.[65] Indeed, a tension emerges between an eschatology that has already been inaugurated by the incarnation, death, and resurrection of Christ, and a future eschatology that will be consummated in the life of the age to come.[66] This is not to say that Christians were nonchalant about the end of history or their own death. Speculation on the Last Judgment as a historical event was common in the sixth century.[67] Romanos draws on this distant yet looming event by cultivating liturgical compunction through his hymns, not simply as a preparation for future death and judgment, but as a mode of interacting with an unfurling reality that was proleptically internalized in the hearts of the faithful through sacred ritual.

[62]Strophe 18.

[63]Ibid.

[64]*On the Infernal Powers* is a "kontakion of compunction" (κοντάκιον κατανυκτικόν) that was chanted during the Thursday of the fifth week of the Lenten fast (the same day that Andrew of Crete's *Great Kanon* was sung). Romanos le Mélode, *Hymnes. Tome IV*, 242. Although Maas and Trypanis entitle this hymn *On the Crucifixion*, I prefer Grosdidier des Matons' title, *On the Infernal Powers*. *On the Victory of the Cross* was associated with the middle of Lent and the Veneration of the Cross.

[65]Meyendorff, *Byzantine Theology*, 218–20. Moreover, it would not be inaccurate to suggest that, for early Christianity, the eschaton became a protean concept. See Brian Daley, *The Hope of the Early Church: A Handbook of Patristic Eschatology* (Cambridge: Cambridge University Press, 1991), 1–5.

[66]See Georges Florovsky, "The Patristic Age and Eschatology: An Introduction," in *Aspects of Church History: Volume Four in the Collected Works of Georges Florovsky* (Belmont: Nordland Publishing Company, 1975), 63–78.

[67]Daley, *The Hope of the Early Church*, 179–84.

On the Infernal Powers and *On the Victory of the Cross* reminded the faithful of the eschaton and the need for repentance by plunging them into the underworld before returning to the salvific power of Christ's crucifixion. Although the scenes and characters from the underworld that feature in these two hymns are not based on a particular biblical narrative, the apocryphal *Gospel of Nikodemos* had gradually embedded the tale of Christ's descent into hades and the character of Satan in the Christian imagination of Late Antiquity.[68] Chanted in the fifth week of the Lenten period, *On the Infernal Powers* begins with an eschatological tone but quickly recapitulates the imagery of healing that other kontakia such as *On the Repentance of the Ninevites* had evoked earlier in the pre-Lenten and early Lenten phase. The dialogue between self and soul in the prelude is provoked by the imminence of death and the omnipresence of the one "who is everywhere present and filling all things."[69] However, Romanos quickly draws the attention of the congregation to the infirmary of Christ, which is a source of health for all of humanity.[70] This sanctuary of healing that Christ's crucifixion has inaugurated becomes the undoing of the powers of hell and causes the devil to cry out in agony as the scene shifts to the underworld:

> "What shall I do to the Son of Mary?
> The Bethlehemite is killing me [. . .]
> The world has been filled with his healings,
> and my insides are afflicted.[71]

The dramatic dialogue that ensues between the devil and his infernal companions is reminiscent of that which takes place between Hades and Satan in *On the Victory of the Cross*, a hymn that was sung on

---

[68]Georgia Frank, "Dialogue and Deliberation: The Sensory Self in the Hymns of Romanos the Melodist," in *Religion and the Self in Antiquity*, ed. David Brakke, Michael L. Satlow, and Steven Weitzman (Bloomington: Indiana University Press, 2005), 171.

[69]The refrain of the hymn *On the Infernal Powers*.

[70]Strophe 1.

[71]Strophe 1, strophe 2.

Wednesday of mid-Lent. While Christ's crucifixion has paradoxically left Hades bitterly wounded and afraid, Satan insists that this is
nothing more than trickery. When Satan realizes his error, he grieves
with Hades, bemoaning their fall and Adam's return. The tree that
they had prepared as the doom of Mary's child has suddenly become
a sanctuary for murderers, publicans, and harlots. Against the back-
drop of an underworld dirge, the faithful sing a song of triumph as
they behold the most unlikely of heroes—the robber—steal the pearl
from the cross and use it as a key to enter "again into paradise."

Concluding Remarks

Romanos' Lenten hymns present sin as a sickness of the soul and
repentance as its remedy. The rhetoric of these hymns seeks to evoke
compunction, which spurred the faithful to the infirmary of spiritual
healing. In retelling the sacred stories that defined the Byzantines,
Romanos' hymns sought to frame and shape a liturgical community
in Constantinople. Poetry, music, and sacred drama showed forth
the compunction of the prodigal son, Lazarus, and other scriptural
figures. Amidst the overarching narrative of the story of salvation
that frames the Lenten journey, Romanos' hymns present the hidden desires of scriptural characters, inviting the faithful to become
part of the sacred drama unfolding before them and to cry tears of
compunction. They also cultivate compunction by dramatizing the
eschaton as a culmination of history that Christ's incarnation, death,
and resurrection had already inaugurated.

The faithful were invited to partake in this liturgical event by
hearing the words and melody of the kontakion and singing the
refrain. Even if a member of the congregation had no talent in
singing, the action of listening to the sacred narrative that a hymn's
performance enacted and hearing the voices of its biblical exemplars
perpetuated a shared world of aural images that were impressed
upon the heart.[72] In this way, the liturgical world that hymnody

[72]Carol Harrison, *The Art of Listening in the Early Church* (Oxford: Oxford
University Press, 2013), 8.

created and the compunction of its protagonists could be internalized by the faithful. Hymns were a means of transforming the soul of the one who sang them. The words and melody of Romanos' protagonists could become more than the utterances of a scriptural character or hymnographer; they could become the voice and confession of the faithful.

Select bibliography

Frank, Georgia. "Romanos and the Night Vigil in the Sixth Century." In *Byzantine Christianity: A People's History of Christianity*, edited by Derek Krueger. Minneapolis: Fortress Press, 2006. Pp. 59–78.

Gador-Whyte, Sarah. *Theology and Poetry in Early Byzantium: The* Kontakia *of Romanos the Melodist*. Cambridge: Cambridge University Press, 2017.

Krueger, Derek. *Liturgical Subjects: Christian Ritual, Biblical Narrative and the Formation of Self in Byzantium*. Philadelphia: University of Pennsylvania Press, 2014.

Mellas, Andrew. *Liturgy and the Emotions in Byzantium: Compunction and Hymnody*. Cambridge: Cambridge University Press, 2020.

Ware, Kallistos. "The Orthodox Experience of Repentance." *Sobornost* 2 (1980): 18–28.

Α

[No title in the Patmos 213 manuscript]

Τῇ δ΄ τῆς α΄ ἑβδομάδος τῶν νηστειῶν,
κοντάκιον κατανυκτικόν, οὗ ἡ ἀκροστιχίς·
τὸν προφήτην Κυρίου Ῥωμανοῦ, ἦχος α΄.

Προοίμιον

Ἀπεγνωσμένην τὴν Νινευὴ προέφθασας,
    ἐπηγγελμένην   τὴν ἀπειλὴν παρήγαγες
    καὶ τὴν ὀργὴν ἐνίκησε   τὸ ἔλεός σου, Κύριε·
σπλαγχνίσθητι καὶ νῦν   ἐπὶ λαὸν καὶ πόλιν σου,
    παλάμῃ κραταιᾷ   τοὺς καθ᾽ ἡμῶν κατάβαλε
    πρεσβείαις τῆς Θεοτόκου,
    προσδεχόμενος ἡμῶν   τὴν μετάνοιαν.

Α

Τὸ ἰατρεῖον τῆς μετανοίας   τοῖς γνώμῃ ἀρρωστοῦσιν ἠνέῳκται·
    δεῦτε,
    προφθάσωμεν,   κἀκεῖθεν ῥῶσιν   ταῖς ψυχαῖς ἡμῶν λάβωμεν·
ἐν αὐτῷ γὰρ ἡ πόρνη ὑγίανεν,
ἐν αὐτῷ ἀπέθετο   καὶ ὁ Πέτρος τὴν ἄρνησιν,

1

On the Repentance of the Ninevites

On Wednesday of the first week of Lent,
a kontakion of compunction, bearing the following acrostic:
Romanos, the prophet of the Lord; first mode.

PRELUDE

O Lord, putting aside the despair of Nineveh,
    you abandoned the threat that had been proclaimed
    and your mercy conquered your anger.[1]
Even now, have pity on your people and your city,
    with your mighty hand strike down those who are against us,
    through the intercession of the Theotokos,
    accepting our repentance.

1

The infirmary of repentance for those who are wilfully sick has
    opened. Come,
let us act in anticipation and let us receive from there strength for
    our souls;
for there the harlot became healthy,[2]
there also Peter put away his denial,[3]

---

[1]Jonah 3.5–10. Old Testament references are to the Septuagint. See Albert Pietersma and Benjamin G. Wright, *A New English Translation of the Septuagint* (New York: Oxford University Press, 2007).
[2]Luke 7.36–50.
[3]John 21.15–19.

ἐν αὐτῷ τὸ ἐγκάρδιον   ἄλγος Δαυὶδ ἔθραυσεν,
    ἐν αὐτῷ καὶ Νινευῆται ἰατρεύθησαν.
Μὴ οὖν ὀκνῶμεν, ἀλλ᾽ ἀναστῶμεν
    καὶ δείξωμεν τὸ τραῦμα   τῷ Σωτῆρι,   καὶ λάβωμεν
    ἔμπλαστρον·
    ὑπὲρ πάντα γὰρ πόθον   **προσδέχεται ἡμῶν   τὴν μετάνοιαν.**

Β

Οὐκ ἀπαιτεῖται μισθὸν οὐδὲ εἷς   τῶν αὐτῷ προσελθόντων
    οὐδέποτε, ὅτι
    οὐκ ἴσχυον   τῆς ἰατρείας   δοῦναι δῶρον ἀντάξιον·
διὰ τοῦτο δωρεὰν ὑγίαιναν,
ἐκεῖνο δὲ ἔδωκαν   ὃ καὶ δοῦναι ἐδύναντο,
ἀντὶ δώρων τὰ δάκρυα·   ἔστι γὰρ καὶ φίλτατα
    καὶ ἐράσμια τῷ ῥύστῃ   καὶ ποθούμενα·
μάρτυς ἡ πόρνη   ἅμα τῷ Πέτρῳ,
    Δαυὶδ καὶ Νινευῆται,   ὅτι μόνον   κλαυθμὸν προσενέγκαντες,
    ὑπέπεσαν τῷ ῥύστῃ,   **καὶ ἐδέξατο αὐτῶν   τὴν μετάνοιαν.**

Γ

Νικᾷ πολλάκις κλαυθμὸς τὸν Θεόν,   εἰ ἔξεστιν εἰπεῖν, καὶ βιάζεται
    ὄντως
    ἡδέως γὰρ   ὑπὸ δακρύων   ὁ οἰκτίρμων συνέχεται,
τῶν δακρύων δὲ τῶν ἐκ τοῦ πνεύματος,
οὐ τῶν ἐκ τοῦ σώματος,   ὧν αἱ θλίψεις παραίτιοι·
καὶ νεκροὺς γὰρ δακρύομεν   καὶ ἐκ πληγῶν κλαίομεν·
    ἡ γὰρ σὰρξ πηλὸς ὑπάρχει   ῥέων ἄπαυστα.
Κλαύσωμεν τοίνυν   ἀπὸ καρδίας,
    ὃν τρόπον Νινευῆται   κατανύξει   τὸν οὐρανὸν ἤνοιξαν
    καὶ ὤφθησαν τῷ ῥύστῃ,   **καὶ ἐδέξατο αὐτῶν   τὴν μετάνοιαν.**

there David broke down the pain of his heart,[4]
    and there the Ninevites were cured.
Let us not be indolent, but let us rise up,
    and let us show our wound to the Savior, let us receive a salve;
    for above every desire, *he accepts our repentance.*

2

The Savior never demands pay, not from even one of those who
    come to him,
    because it is not possible to give a gift worthy of the cure;
therefore, they were becoming healthy for free.
But they gave the only thing they were able to give:
tears instead of gifts. For tears are cherished, beloved, and desired
    by the deliverer.
The harlot is a witness to this and so is Peter,
    David, and the Ninevites, because having only offered weeping,
    they fell down before the Savior *and he accepted their*
    repentance.

3

If it is lawful to say, weeping often overcomes God, for truly
    the compassionate one is pleasantly constrained by tears,
by tears that are from the soul,
not from the body, tears that are partly caused by afflictions.
For we not only weep over the dead but also cry from wounds;
    for our flesh is clay, flowing with unceasing tears.
Therefore, let us weep from the heart,
    in which manner the Ninevites, with compunction, opened
    heaven and they were seen by the deliverer, *and he accepted*
    their repentance.

[4]2 Reigns 12.13 (2 Samuel 12.13).

Δ

Περὶ οὖν τούτους εἰλήσθω ὁ νοῦς· αὐτῶν γὰρ καὶ ἔστιν ἡ
  ὑπόθεσις ὅθεν
  σχολάσωμεν, καὶ τῶν ἐκείνοις πεπραγμένων ἀκούσωμεν.
Μετ᾽ ἐκεῖνο τὸ ἔμφοβον κήρυγμα
ὃ πρώην ἐκήρυξε Ἰωνᾶς τοῖς μὴ νήφουσι,
μετ᾽ ἐκείνην τὴν ἄστεκτον καὶ τὴν ἀνυπόστατον
  ἀπειλὴν ἦν ὁ προφήτης προεκήρυξεν,
οἱ Νινευῆται ὥσπερ τεχνῖται
  ἐπιστηρίξαι πόλιν ἣν κακίαι ἐσάλευσαν ἔσπευσαν,
  οὐ λίθον ὑποθέντες, **ἀλλὰ πέτραν ἀσφαλῆ τὴν μετάνοιαν.**

Ε

Ῥοαῖς δακρύων τὸν ῥύπον αὐτῆς ἐκπλύναντες εὐχαῖς
  κατεκόσμησαν ὅλην,
  καὶ ἤρεσεν ἐπιστραφεῖσα Νινευὴ τῷ οἰκτίρμονι·
τὸ γὰρ κάλλος αὐτῆς τὸ ἐγκάρδιον
εὐθέως ὑπέδειξε τῷ καρδίας ἐτάζοντι,
καὶ τὴν σάρκα τὴν ἄμορφον σάκκῳ σποδῷ μίξασα,
  εὐποιΐαις ὡς ἐλαίῳ ἐπεχρίσατο,
καὶ ταῖς νηστείαις μυρισαμένη
  πρὸς τὸν ἀρχαῖον ἄνδρα ἀναλύει καὶ τούτῳ προσπλέκεται,
  διὸ καὶ ὁ νυμφίος **ἠγκαλίσατο αὐτῆς τὴν μετάνοιαν.**

ΣΤ

Ὁ βασιλεὺς δὲ αὐτῆς ὁ σοφός, καθάπερ νυμφοστόλος γενόμενος,
  τότε ἐκέλευσε τὴν πόλιν πᾶσαν ἀρετὴν ἀναδήσασθαι,
καὶ ὡς νύμφην λοιπὸν ἐκαλλώπισε,
καὶ κτήνη καὶ θρέμματα ὡς εἰς φερνὴν ηὐτρέπιζε,

4

Therefore, let the mind internalize these Ninevites, for they are the
    subject to which
we should be devoted, and let us hear what has happened to them.
After that terrible proclamation,[5]
which Jonah previously preached to those who were not temperate,
after that unbearable and irresistible
    threat, which the prophet preached beforehand,
the Ninevites, like craftsmen,
    hastened to strengthen the city, which evils shook,
    not having laid down a stone, *but the firm rock of repentance.*

5

Having washed away the filth of the city with streams of tears, they
    adorned the entire city with prayers,
    and Nineveh, having converted to the compassionate one,
    pleased him;
for she immediately showed the beauty in her heart to the one who
    examines the heart,
and having mingled the misshapen flesh with sackcloth and ashes,
    she anointed it with beneficence as with oil,
and having poured the perfume of fastings on it,
    she returns toward the ancient husband and is united with him,
wherefore the Bridegroom *embraced her repentance.*

6

The wise king of the city, having become like one who escorts the
    bride, then commanded the entire city to be crowned with
    virtue,
and, as a bride, he embellished her further,
and he was preparing cattle and herds as her dowry,

[5]Jonah 3.4.

«Πάντα, λέγων, προσφέρω σοι· μόνον διαλλάγηθι,
   νυμφίε, Θεέ, σωτήρ μου, καταλλάγηθι
τῇ πορνευσάσῃ καὶ ἀποστάσῃ
   ἐκ τῆς ἀκηλιδώτου συνουσίας τῆς σῆς καθαρότητος·
   ἰδοὺ γάρ σε φιλοῦσα **σοὶ προσφέρει δωρεὰν τὴν μετάνοιαν.**

Z

Φωνὴ ἀλόγων ζητούντων νομήν· ἀνθρώποις γὰρ ὁμοῦ καὶ τοῖς
   κτήνεσι πᾶσιν
   ἐκέλευσα νηστείαν ἄγειν ἕως ἂν φιλιωθῇς ἡμῖν.
Εἰ ἐγὼ ὁ ἀνάσσων ἠνόμησα,
ἐμὲ μόνον ἔτασον καὶ τοὺς πάντας ἐλέησον·
εἰ δὲ πάντες ἡμάρτομεν, πάντων φωνὰς ἄκουσον,
   τῶν βοῶν καὶ τῶν προβάτων τὰ μυκήματα
καὶ τῶν ἀνθρώπων τὰς ἱκεσίας·
   ἐπιφθασάτω μόνον ἡ ῥοπή σου, καὶ πᾶν δεινὸν λέλυται·
   οὐ δειλιῶμεν φόβον, **ἐὰν δέξῃ παρ' ἡμῶν τὴν μετάνοιαν.**

H

Ἡ τὸν ζυγόν σου, σῶτερ ἀγαθέ, τραχήλου ἑαυτῆς ἀπορρίψασα
   αὕτη
   προσπίπτει σοι καὶ πάλιν τοῦτον ὑποθεῖναι ἐπείγεται·
Νινευὴ ἡ δραπέτις προσπίπτει σοι,
κἀγὼ ὁ ταλαίπωρος βασιλεὺς καὶ οἰκέτης σου,
ὡς τοῦ θρόνου ἀνάξιος ἐπὶ σποδοῦ κάθημαι,
   ὡς τὸ στέμμα καθυβρίσας κόνιν πέπασμαι,
ὡς μὴ ἁρμόζων τῇ πορφυρίδῃ
   τὸν σάκκον ἐνεδύθην καὶ ὠδυνήθην· διὸ μὴ παρίδῃς με·
   ἐπίβλεψον, σωτήρ μου, **καὶ πρόσδεξαι ἡμῶν τὴν μετάνοιαν.**

saying: "I offer all things to you; only be reconciled,
  O Bridegroom, O God, O my Savior, reconcile
with her who became a prostitute and apostate
    from the undefiled intercourse with your purity.
    For behold, kissing you, *she freely offers you repentance.*

7

"The cry of beasts seeking pasture![6] I commanded the people,
    together with all the animals,
    to observe the fast until you befriend us.
If I, the one who rules, acted lawlessly,
try me alone and have mercy on all the people;
but if we all sinned, hear the voices of all,
    the roars of the oxen and the sheep
and the supplications of the people.
    Let only your divine help arrive, and every terrible thing will
      have been brought to an end.
    Let us not be afraid of that which causes terror, *if you accept our
    repentance.*

8

"O good Savior, the city who has thrown aside your yoke from her
    neck,
    she falls before you in supplication, hastening to pledge herself
    again to you.
Nineveh, the runaway slave, falls down before you in supplication,
    and I, your wretched king and servant,
as one unworthy of the throne, I sit upon ashes,
as one who dishonored the crown, I have sprinkled myself with
    dust, as one who is not fit for the purple,
I was clothed in sackcloth and I suffered torment. Therefore, do
    not overlook me; look favorably upon me, O my Savior,
    and accept my repentance."

[6]Jeremiah 32.36.

Θ

Τίς ὠφελία ἐν τῇ Νινευῇ   ἐὰν καταστραφῇ, ἀναμάρτητε μόνε;
   Μὴ δύναται ὁ χοῦς ἐν Ἅιδῃ ἀναγγεῖλαί σοι αἴνεσιν;
Διὰ τοῦτο οἱ ζῶντες ζητοῦμέν σε·
ἐκεῖνο ὃ πέφυκας, τοῦτο δεῖξον τοῖς δούλοις σου·
ἐλεήμων, οἰκτίρμων εἶ, οἴκτειρον, ἐλέησον·
   μὴ ποιήσῃς ἡμᾶς πῆμα τῶν ἐχθρῶν ἡμῶν,
μὴ μισηθῶμεν ὡς Σοδομῖται,
     μὴ γέλως ἐξαπίνης τοῖς ἐχθροῖς μου ἡ πόλις σου γένηται,
     ἀλλὰ ὡς ἐλεήμων **νῦν πρόσδεξαι ἡμῶν** **τὴν μετάνοιαν.**

Ι

Ἡ ναυαγοῦσα ὁλκὰς Νινευὴ καὶ πάσης τῆς ζωῆς ἀπελπίσασα,
   κράξον
   καὶ αἴτησαι τὸν πάντων ῥύστην δεξιὰν ἐπιδοῦναί σοι·
ὁ γὰρ σὲ κυβερνῶν οὐκ ἀκούομαι·
πάντων γὰρ τὰ πταίσματα ἐν ἐμοὶ μόνῳ φαίνεται.
Διὰ τοῦτο οὖν κραύγασον· τάχα τοῖς σοῖς πείθεται
   καὶ τοῖς δάκρυσί σου μᾶλλον ἐπικάμπτεται·
κλαῦσον, ὦ νύμφη, κλαύσατε, νέοι,
     κλαύσατε, νεανίσκος σὺν παρθένῳ, πρεσβῦται καὶ νήπια,
     ἐνώπιον Κυρίου **προσενέγκωμεν** **τὴν μετάνοιαν.**»

ΙΑ

Νομοθετήσας τοιαῦτά ποτε ὁ πάνσοφος ὁμοῦ καὶ πανεύφημος
   ἄναξ
   ὑπήκοον τὴν πόλιν πᾶσαν εὗρεν, ὥσπερ ἠθέλησε.
Καὶ μαστῶν ὁ θηλάζων ἀπείχετο,

9

"O only sinless one, what benefit is there in Nineveh if it is
   destroyed? Is the dust in hades able to proclaim a song of praise
   to you?[7]
Therefore, we the living seek you;
that which you have begotten, show this to your servants.
O merciful one, being compassionate, show compassion and have
   mercy; may you not make us the prey of our enemies,
let us not be hated as the Sodomites,[8]
   let not your city suddenly become an object of laughter for
   my enemies, but as one who is merciful, *accept now our
   repentance.*"

10

"Nineveh, the trading vessel that is suffering shipwreck and has
   despaired of all life, cry out
   and ask the deliverer of all to extend his right hand to you;
for I who govern you am not heard,
for the errors of all appear only in me.
Therefore, cry out; perhaps he is persuaded by your prayers
   and he bends all the more to your tears.
Weep, O bride, weep, O young men,
   weep, youth together with virgin, old men and infants,
   in the presence of the Lord, *let us bring our repentance.*"

11

The all-wise and all-praiseworthy king, having once instructed
   them in such things,
   found the whole city obedient, just as he wished.
The one who was suckling abstained from the breasts,

[7]Psalm 6.6.
[8]Genesis 13.13, 19.24.

παῖδες ἀσεβήσαντες ἡδονῶν ἀπετάξαντο,
καὶ τὸν γάμον τὰ γύναια τίμιον ἡγήσαντο,
  καὶ ἀμίαντον τὴν κοίτην διεφύλαξαν·
πάντες οἱ νέοι ἅμα πρεσβύταις
  εὐχαῖς, λιταῖς, νηστείαις, εὐποιΐαις τὸν νῶτον συνέκαμψαν,
  καὶ ταῦτα αὐτῶν πραξάντων **προσεδέξατο ὁ Θεὸς τὴν
  μετάνοιαν.**

ΙΒ

Καὶ ἵνα γνῶμεν τὸ μεῖζον καλόν, οὐκ εἶπεν ἡ γραφὴ ὅτι ἤσκησαν
  μόνον,
  οὐδ᾽ ἔφησεν ὅτι νηστείαις καὶ τῷ σάκκῳ ἐχρήσαντο,
ἀλλὰ τί μετὰ ταῦτα ἐποίησαν·
ἐβόησεν ἕκαστος ἐκτενῶς πρὸς τὸν Κύριον,
πρὸς ἐκεῖνον ἔφυγον πάλιν ἐπανέλυσαν·
  οὐ γὰρ εὗρον ἄλλον οὕτω σπλαγχνιζόμενον,
μετανοοῦντα ἐπὶ κακίαις
  καὶ ἀγαπῶντα σώζειν καὶ φιλοῦντα λυτροῦσθαι καὶ ῥύεσθαι
  καὶ σπεύδοντα οἰκτείρειν **καὶ δεχόμενον αὐτῶν τὴν
  μετάνοιαν.**

ΙΓ

Ὑπὸ δὲ τούτων εὐθὺς Ἰωνᾶς τῇ λύπῃ ἑαυτὸν κατεμάρανε λέγων·
  «Οὐκ ἔλεγον ὅτι οἰκτείρεις καὶ οὐ κτείνεις, φιλόψυχε·
διὰ τοῦτο γὰρ φεύγειν ἐσπούδαζον,
οὐχ ἵνα [μὴ] πέμψῃς με, ἀλλὰ ἵνα μὴ ψεύσωμαι·
καὶ τὰ νῦν ἠθύμησα, οὐκ ἐπειδὴ ἔσωσας,
  ἀλλ᾽ ἐζήτουν· «Ὡς τῶν πρώτων κήρυξ γέγονα,
οὕτως καὶ τούτων ἀξιωθείην.»
  Ἀλλ᾽ ἐγενόμην κήρυξ τῆς ὀργῆς σου καὶ οὐ τῆς ἀφέσεως·
  ἐγὼ σκληρὸς οἰκέτης, **σὺ δὲ πρᾶος καὶ φιλόστοργος.**

impious children took leave of pleasures,
weak women regarded marriage as honorable
   and kept the marriage-bed undefiled.[9]
All the youths together with the old men
   bent their backs in prayers, supplications, fasts, and good deeds,
   and, having done these things, *God accepted their repentance.*

12

And so that we might know the greater good, Scripture
   did not say that they only practiced asceticism,
   nor did it just say that they made use of fasts and sackcloth,
but what did they do after these things?
Each person cried out fervently to the Lord,
toward him they returned again, to the one they turned from;
   for they did not find another having such compassion,
repenting of evils,[10]
   loving to save, to redeem, and to deliver,
   and hastening to have compassion *and accepting their
   repentance.*

13

By means of these things, Jonah immediately languished with
   grief, saying: "Did I not say, O Lover of souls, that you feel
   compassion and do not kill?
For because of this I was hastening to leave,
not so that you might not send me, but so that I might not lie.
And now I am disheartened, not because you saved them,
   but because I was seeking to become the herald of the most
   important things, and thus be deemed worthy of them.
But I became a herald of your wrath and not of forgiveness;
   I, a callous servant, *but you, gentle and loving.*"

[9]Hebrews 13.4.
[10]Jonah 3.10.

ΙΔ

Ῥανίδα μόνην τῶν σῶν οἰκτιρμῶν   παράσχου μοι τὰ νῦν ὡς οἰκέτῃ
    σου· λάβε
    τὸ πνεῦμα μου·   καλὸν γάρ ἐστι   τὸ θανεῖν ἢ τὸ ζῆσαί με.»
Καὶ τοιαῦτα εἰπὼν ἐκαθεύδησε·
    τῇ λύπῃ γὰρ πάντοτε   καὶ ὁ ὕπνος ἀκόλουθος.
Ὁ δὲ μόνος ἀνύστακτος   τότε τὸν κοιμώμενον
    τῇ σκιᾷ τῆς κολοκύντης   ἐπανέπαυσε,
ταύτῃ σκεπάζων   τὸν ἀθυμοῦντα
    καὶ δι᾽ αὐτῆς διδάσκων   τὸν προφήτην   μισεῖν τὸ ἀπότομον
    καὶ ἅπασι συμπάσχειν   **καὶ φιλεῖν   τὴν μετάνοιαν.**

ΙΕ

Ἰδοὺ ὁ τύπος τοῦ νόμου σαφῶς   ἐπὶ τῆς κολοκύντης γνωρίζεται
    ὄντως·
    φυεῖσα γὰρ   νυκτὸς ἐκείνη   Ἰωνᾶν ὑπεσκίαζε·
καὶ ὁ νόμος σκιάζων τὰ μέλλοντα
νυκτὸς ἀνεβλάστησε   τῷ Μωσεῖ ὑπονέφελα·
ἡ δὲ χάρις ὡς ἥλιος   ἄρτι ἀνατείλασα
    ἐπεκάλυψε τὸν νόμον   ὡς τὸ λάχανον.
Ὅθεν ὁ κόσμος, ὡς ὁ προφήτης,
    ἀφυπνισθεὶς κατεῖδεν   ὅτι πᾶσαν   τοῦ νόμου τὴν ἄγρωστιν
    ἐθέρισεν ἡ χάρις,   **καὶ ἐφύτευσεν ἡμῖν   τὴν μετάνοιαν.**

ΙΣΤ

Ὁ μὲν προφήτης ποτὲ Ἰωνᾶς   ἐχάρη κατιδὼν τὴν κολόκυνταν
    τότε,
    καὶ ἄθροον   ὡς ξηρανθεῖσαν   θεωρήσας ἠθύμησεν.
Ὁ δὲ πλάστης φησὶ πρὸς τὸν ὅσιον·
«Εἰ σφόδρα λελύπησαι   ὑπὲρ ἧς οὐκ ἐκοπίασας,

14

"Grant me now, as your servant, only a drop of your compassions; receive
   my spirit, for it is better for me to die rather than to live."[11]
And having said such things, he slept;
for sleep always follows grief.
But then, the one who alone is vigilant rested the one falling asleep
   under the shade of the gourd,
covering the disheartened Jonah with the shade,
   and through the gourd, teaching the prophet to hate severe
   punishment, to have sympathy for all *and to love repentance.*

15

Behold, clearly a type of the law is truly made known by the gourd;
   for growing by night, it was gradually overshadowing Jonah.
And the law, overshadowing the things to come,[12]
sprouted by night to Moses under the clouds;
but grace, dawning now like the sun,
   covered the law as one puts a cover over a garden herb.
Therefore, the world, like the prophet,
   having been woken from sleep, perceived that grace mowed all
   the dog's tooth grass of the law, *and planted for us repentance.*

16

At one time, having beheld the gourd, Jonah rejoiced.
   At another time, when the gourd suddenly withered, having
   seen it he became disheartened.
But the Creator said to the holy man:
"If you are exceedingly grieved over the gourd,

[11]Jonah 4.3.
[12]Hebrews 10.1.

εἰ τὸ ἄνθος σε ἔθλιψε,   πόσῳ μᾶλλον ἄνθρωπος;
   Εἰ τοῦ χόρτου ξηρανθέντος   ὠλιγώρησας,
μὴ οἰκτείρω πόλιν τὴν τοιαύτην
   ἐν μέτρῳ δεκαδύο   μυριάδας   ἀνδρῶν πλήρης γέμουσαν;
   Διὸ μεγαλοψύχει   **καὶ ἀγάπα σὺν ἡμῖν   τὴν μετάνοιαν.**»

ΙΖ

Υἱὲ τοῦ μόνου καὶ μόνε Θεέ,   ὁ θέλημα ποιῶν τῶν φιλούντων σε,
   ῥῦσαι
   ὡς εὔσπλαγχνος   ἐκ τῆς μελλούσης   ἀπειλῆς, ἀναμάρτητε·
ὥς ποτε Νινευήτας ᾠκτείρησας
καὶ τῶν μυστηρίων σου   Ἰωνᾶν κατηξίωσας,
οὕτω νῦν τοὺς ὑμνοῦντάς σε   λύτρωσαι τῆς κρίσεως,
   καὶ ἐμοὶ μισθὸν τοῦ λόγου   δὸς τὴν ἄφεσιν·
λέγειν γὰρ οἶδα,   πράττειν δ’ οὐκ οἶδα·
   ἐπειδὴ οὖν οὐκ ἔχω   ἔργα, σῶτερ,   τῆς σῆς δόξης ἄξια,
   ἀλλ’ οὖν διὰ τοὺς λόγους   **ἐξελοῦ με φιλῶν   τὴν μετάνοιαν.**

for which you did not toil, if the blossom afflicted you, how much
    more so should you grieve over a human being?
If you were discouraged by the withered vegetation, should I not
    have compassion on a city such as this one, a city completely
    full in the measure of a hundred and twenty thousand people?[13]
    Therefore, be generous *and, together with us, love repentance.*"

17

O Son of the only God, and only God, the one who creates the will
    of those who love you, as one who is tender-hearted,
deliver us from the coming threat, O sinless one.
As you once had compassion on the Ninevites
and deemed Jonah worthy of your mysteries,
in the same way now redeem from judgment those who sing a
    hymn to you, and grant to me forgiveness as a reward for the
    homily;
for I know how to speak, but I do not know how to act.
    Therefore, O Savior, because I do not have works worthy of
    your glory, nevertheless, through my words, *deliver me, O lover*
    of repentance.

[13]Jonah 4.9–11.

B

[No title in the Patmos 213 manuscript]

Τῇ δ' τῆς β' ἑβδομάδος τῶν νηστειῶν· κοντάκιον
κατανυκτικόν. Φέρον ἀκροστιχίδα τήνδε·
τοῦ ταπεινοῦ Ῥωμανοῦ ὁ ὕμνος
ἦχος α', πρός· Τὸ ἰατρεῖον τῆς μετανοίας.

Προοίμιον

Σχόλασον, ψυχή μου, ἐν μετανοίᾳ,
    ἑνώθητι Χριστῷ κατὰ γνώμην,
    βοῶσα ἐν στεναγμοῖς·
«Συγχώρησιν παράσχου μοι
    τῶν δεινῶν μου πράξεων,
    ἵνα λάβω παρὰ σοῦ, μόνε ἀγαθέ,
    τὴν ἄφεσιν καὶ ζωὴν τὴν αἰώνιον.»

Α

Τῆς μακαρίας τυχεῖν ἐλπίδος   δι᾽ ἔργων προσδοκῶμεν καὶ
    πίστεως, ὅσοι
    φυλάττομεν   τὰ τοῦ Κυρίου   καὶ σωτῆρος διδάγματα·
διὰ τοῦτο τιμῶμεν καὶ στέργομεν
τὸ ἀγγέλοις τίμιον   τῆς νηστείας κατόρθωμα,
ὃ προφῆται τηρήσαντες   μέτοχοι γεγόνασι
    τῶν χορῶν τῶν οὐρανίων,   οἱ ἐπίγειοι,

2

On Fasting

On Wednesday of the second week of Lent,
a kontakion of compunction, bearing the following acrostic:
the hymn of the humble Romanos.
First mode, according to: "The infirmary of repentance."

PRELUDE

O my soul, devote yourself to repentance,
    be willingly united to Christ,
    crying out with groans,
"O only Good One, grant me forgiveness
    for my terrible deeds,
    that I may receive from you,
    forgiveness and eternal life."

1

Let us expect the blessed hope[1] through works and faith, as many
    of us as
    observe the teachings of the Lord and Savior.
That is why we honor and love
the achievement of fasting, which is honored by angels,
by keeping it, the earthly prophets became partners
    of the heavenly choirs,

[1]Titus 2.13.

ὅπου γε ταύτης   τὴν ἐργασίαν
   Χριστὸς οὐκ ἐπῃσχύνθη   ἐκτελέσαι· ἑκὼν δὲ ἐνήστευσεν,
ἡμῖν καθυπογράφων   διὰ ταύτης **τὴν ζωὴν   τὴν αἰώνιον.**

Β

Ὅτι μεγάλοι ἐν ἔργοις ἦσαν   Μωσῆς καὶ Ἠλίας οἱ πύρινοι πύργοι
   γινώσκομεν,   ὅτι καὶ πρῶτοι   ἐν προφήταις τυγχάνουσι,
πρὸς Θεὸν παρρησίαν ἐκέκτηντο,
ὅτιπερ ἐβούλοντο   προσιέναι καὶ δέεσθαι
καὶ αὐτῷ διαλέγεσθαι   πρόσωπον πρὸς πρόσωπον,
   ὃ ὑπάρχει θαυμαστόν τε   καὶ παράδοξον.
Ὅμως καὶ οὕτως   πρὸς τὴν νηστείαν
   κατέφευγον σπουδαίως,   διὰ ταύτης   αὐτῷ προσαγόμενοι·
νηστεία οὖν μετ᾽ ἔργων   **ἀποδίδωσι ζωὴν   τὴν αἰώνιον.**

Γ

Ὑπὸ νηστείας ὡς ὑπὸ ξίφους   οἱ δαίμονες πάντες ἐλαύνονται ὅτι
   οὐ φέρουσιν   οὐδ᾽ ἐξαρκοῦσι   πρὸς τὴν ταύτης τερπνότητα·
τρυφητὴν ἀγαπῶσι καὶ μέθυσον·
ἐὰν δὲ θεάσωνται   τῆς νηστείας τὸ πρόσωπον,
οὔτε στῆναι ἰσχύουσι·   πόρρω δὲ ἐκτρέχουσιν,
   ὡς Χριστὸς ἡμᾶς διδάσκει   ὁ Θεὸς ἡμῶν
λέγων· «Τὸ γένος   τὸ τῶν δαιμόνων
   νηστείᾳ καὶ δεήσει   ἐκνικᾶται.»   Διὸ δεδιδάγμεθα
ὡς δίδωσι νηστεία   **τοῖς ἀνθρώποις ζωὴν   τὴν αἰώνιον.**

Δ

Τῆς σωφροσύνης ἁγνεία μήτηρ   ὑπάρχει τῆς νηστείας τὸ
   ἄχραντον κάλλος·
   πηγάζει δὲ   φιλοσοφίαν   καὶ παρέχει τὸν στέφανον·

since indeed Christ was not ashamed to accomplish this work; he
    fasted willingly,[2]
    underwriting for us through this *eternal life.*

2

That Moses and Elias, those fiery towers, were great in works we
    know, and that they are first among prophets,
they obtained the right to say freely to God
whatever they wished, to approach him
and entreat him and to talk with him face to face,[3]
    something that is wonderful and paradoxical.
Nevertheless, they also earnestly resorted to fasting,
    because of this they were brought to him.
      Therefore, fasting with works *restores eternal life.*

3

By fasting as by a sword all the demons are routed, because
    they cannot bear nor do they have strength against its delight.
They love pleasure-seekers and drunkards;
but if they see the face of fasting,
they cannot hold their ground, but flee far away,
    as Christ our God teaches us
when he says, "The race of demons
    is vanquished by fasting and prayer."[4] And so,
    we have been taught that fasting *gives people eternal life.*

4

The holy mother of sound judgment is the immaculate beauty of
    fasting:
    it overflows with philosophy and grants the crown;

[2]Matthew 4.2.
[3]Deuteronomy 5.4; Sirach 45.5.
[4]Matthew 17.21; Mark 9.29.

προξενεῖ δὲ ἡμῖν τὸν παράδεισον,
τὴν πατρῴαν δίδωσιν οἰκιὰν τοῖς νηστεύουσιν,
ἧς ὁ Ἀδὰμ ἀπωλίσθησεν· εἵλκυσε δὲ θάνατον,
    ἀτιμάσας τῆς νηστείας τὸ ἀξίωμα·
ταύτης γὰρ τότε καθυβρισθείσης,
    Θεὸς ὁ πάντων κτίστης καὶ δεσπότης εὐθὺς ἠγανάκτησε
    τοῖς ταύτην δὲ τιμῶσιν **ἀποδίδωσι ζωὴν τὴν αἰώνιον.**

Ε

Αὐτὸς γάρ, ὡς μητρὶ φιλοστόργῳ, νηστείας ἐντολῇ ὁ
    φιλάνθρωπος πρώην
    παρέθετο ὡς διδασκάλῳ παραχθέντα τὸν ἄνθρωπον,
ἐν χερσὶν παραδοὺς τὴν ζωὴν αὐτοῦ·
καὶ εἰ ταύτην ἔστερξε, μετ᾽ ἀγγέλων ηὐλίζετο·
ἀθετήσας δὲ εὕρετο πόνους καὶ τὸν θάνατον,
    ἀκανθῶν δὲ καὶ τριβόλων τὴν τραχύτητα
καὶ ἐπιμόχθου βίου τὴν θλῖψιν.
    Εἰ δὲ ἐν παραδείσῳ νηστεία ὠφέλιμος δείκνυται,
    πόσῳ μᾶλλον ἐνταῦθα, **ἵνα σχῶμεν τὴν ζωὴν τὴν αἰώνιον.**

ΣΤ

Παντὸς μὲν ξύλου κελεύει φαγεῖν τὸν ἄνθρωπον Ἀδὰμ τὸν
    πρωτόπλαστον τότε
    ὁ ὕψιστος ἐν παραδείσῳ θεὶς αὐτόν, καθὼς γέγραπται·
ἀλλ᾽ ἑνὸς ξύλου βρῶσιν ἐκώλυσε·
καὶ αὐτὰ τὰ ῥήματα τὰ τοῦ κτίστου φιλάνθρωπα·
«Κατατρύφα γάρ, ἔλεγε, πάντων ὧν κεχάρισμαι·
    τῇ τρυφῇ γάρ σου τῇ τούτων ἀρεσθήσομαι·
ἐὰν φυλάξῃς τὴν ἐντολήν μου,
    φυλάξω σε τρυφῶντα· διὰ τοῦτο φθορᾶς ἀνεπίδεκτον
    ἡ χάρις μου φρουρεῖ σε ὡς λαμβάνοντα **τὴν ἄφεσιν καὶ
ζωὴν τὴν αἰώνιον.**

it gains us paradise;
it gives to those who fast the ancestral home,
which Adam lost. By dishonoring the dignity of fasting
    he brought in death;
for when God, the creator and master of all,
    saw that fasting had been dishonored, he was at once enraged,
    but to those who honor it *he restores eternal life.*

5

For the Lover of humankind himself once entrusted the
    commandment of fasting, as a loving mother, as a teacher, to
    the human that had been created,
giving life to its hands;
and had he loved it, he would have made his home with angels.
When he set it aside he found toils and death,
    the roughness of thorns and thistles
the affliction of a toilsome life.
    If then in paradise fasting is shown to be useful,
    how much more here, *that we may have eternal life.*

6

The Most High told Adam, the first-formed human, to eat of every
    tree,[5]
    having placed him in paradise, as it is written;
but from one tree he forbade food,
and these were the loving words of the Creator:
"Enjoy," he said, "everything I have given you,
    for I shall be pleased at your enjoyment of them.
If you observe my commandment,
I will preserve you in your enjoyment; my grace will guard you
    and you will be incapable of experiencing corruption, as one
    receiving *forgiveness and eternal life.*

    [5]Genesis 2.16.

Z

Ἐμῶν ῥημάτων ἀνάσχου, Ἀδάμ, καὶ πρόσχες ἀκριβῶς τῷ
προστάγματι τούτῳ·
ἑνὸς γάρ σοι ἐκ πάντων τούτων παραγγέλλω ἀπέχεσθαι,
οὐ κακοῦ μὲν τὴν φύσιν ὑπάρχοντος,
ἀλλὰ σοὶ τὴν κάκωσιν παραβάντι σκευάζοντος.
Ἡ οὐσία τοῦ ξύλου γὰρ ἔστι μὲν οὐκ ἄχρηστος,
ἡ δὲ τούτου μετουσία σοι γενήσεται
βλάβης αἰτία· ἔχει γὰρ τοῦτο
ἀκόνην λογισμῶν ἐγκεκρυμμένην καὶ γεύσεως μάχαιραν·
ἂν φάγῃς οὖν ἐκ τούτου, **ἀποβάλλει τὴν ἄφεσιν καὶ ζωὴν τὴν
αἰώνιον.**

H

Ἰδού, πρωτόπλαστε, παραγγέλλω μὴ ἅψῃ ἐκ τοῦ ξύλου οὗ εἶπόν
σοι ὅλως·
ἂν ἅψῃ γάρ, εὐθὺς ὡς κλέπτης ἐκδοθήσει πρὸς θάνατον,
οὐχ ὡς ἔχειν αὐτὸ μὴ δυνάμενος,
ἀλλ᾽ ἐπειδὴ ἄπιστος ἀποβήσει καὶ ἄχρηστος·
πρὸς μικρόν σε καὶ εὔκολον θεῖον νόμον ἤγαγον·
διὰ τοῦτο τὴν τῶν ἄλλων ἀφθονίαν σοι
ἐδωρησάμην, ἵν᾽ ὅλων τούτων
ἐν ἀπολαύσει γένῃ καὶ θανάτου μὴ γένῃ ὑπεύθυνος,
ὁ κατ᾽ εἰκόνα ἔχων **καὶ κατέχων ζωὴν τὴν αἰώνιον.»**

Θ

Νόμον οὖν θεῖον κρατοῦντές ποτε, Ἀδάμ τε καὶ ἡ Εὔα ἐφύλαττον
τοῦτον·
ἐτήρει δὲ ὁρμὰς τὰς τούτων ὁ διάβολος

7

"Hold fast to my words, Adam, and pay close attention to this
command;

of all these things I order you to abstain from only one,[6]
not that it is bad by nature,
but if you disobey, it will be the instrument of your misfortune.
For the essence of the tree is not useless,

but partaking of it will for you
be a cause of harm; for it possesses

a hidden whetstone for thoughts and a knife for the taste;
Therefore, if you eat of it, *you throw away forgiveness and eternal
life.*"

8

"Behold, O first-formed,[7] I command you not even to touch the
tree of which I told you;

for if you touch it, at once like a thief, you will be given over to
death,

not that you cannot have it,
but because you will prove to be faithless and useless.
I have brought you to a small and easy divine law,

and, therefore, I have given you the abundance
of other things, so that of all these you may take your delight and
not become subject to death, you who,

as the image of God,[8] have *and possess eternal life.*"

9

Therefore, holding firmly to the law of God, Adam and Eve began
by keeping it;

but the devil was watching their inclinations,

[6]Genesis 2.17.
[7]Wisdom of Solomon 7.1, 10.1.
[8]Genesis 1.26–27.

καὶ ἀπάτην σκευάζειν ἐπείγετο,
καὶ ὡς ἐθεάσατο κρυπτομένους ὡς ἔμφρονας,
προσελθεῖν τῷ ἀνθρώπῳ μὲν τέως οὐκ ἐθάρρησε·
 τὴν δὲ Εὔαν ὁ πανοῦργος θεασάμενος
παρὰ τὸ δένδρον μόνην ἑστῶσαν,
 ἐντίθησιν εὐθέως διὰ ταύτης τοῖς δύο τὸ πρόσκομμα
τοῖς πρότερον λαβοῦσι **διὰ χάριτος ζωὴν τὴν αἰώνιον.**

I

Ὁ πονηρὸς γὰρ πρὸς τὴν γυναῖκα ὡς φίλος καὶ συνήθης
 προσέρχεται δόλῳ
 καὶ πλάττεται καὶ προκομίζει τὴν κακοῦργον ἐρώτησιν·
ὡς συμπάσχων αὐτῇ διαλέγεται·
«Διὰ ποίαν πρόφασιν ὁ Θεὸς τὸν παράδεισον
ὡς φιλῶν ὑμῖν δέδωκε, πάντων δὲ ἐκώλυσε
 τῶν φυτῶν μεταλαμβάνειν ὁ φιλότιμος;
Τίνος οὖν χάριν τοῦ παραδείσου
 τὴν οἴκησιν κρατεῖτε, τῆς δὲ τούτου τρυφῆς ἐστερήθητε;
 Πῶς δύνασθε οὖν ἔχειν **ζωὴν τὴν αἰώνιον;»**

IA

Ὑπὸ τῶν λόγων ἀπατηθεῖσα, ἡ Εὔα πρὸς αὐτὸν ἀπεκρίνατο
 ταῦτα·
 «Πεπλάνησαι καὶ οὐ γινώσκεις τί προσέταξε Κύριος.
Τὸν παράδεισον ὅλον ὡς τράπεζαν
παραχθεῖσι δέδωκεν ὁ Θεὸς εἰς ἀπόλαυσιν,
ἀλλ᾽ ἑνὸς τὴν μετάληψιν μόνον διεκώλυσεν,
 ἐμποδίου γενομένου τῇ ζωῇ ἡμῶν,
ὃ χρησιμεύει τοῖς ἀμφοτέροις
 καὶ ἐκπαιδεύειν οἶδε τῶν καλῶν τε καὶ φαύλων τὴν εἴδησιν·
 ἐλάβομεν γὰρ ἤδη **ὥσπερ κτῆσιν ζωὴν τὴν αἰώνιον».**

and hastened to prepare a trap,
and when he saw that they were wisely hidden,
for a while he did not dare to approach the man;
  but when the devious one saw Eve
standing alone by the tree,
  through her he at once laid the stumbling block for the two who
  had earlier received *through grace eternal life.*

10

For the wicked one by guile approaches the woman like a friend
  and a familiar,
  and he weaves and produces his cunning question.
As though sympathizing, he talks with her,
"For what reason has God given you paradise,
as though he loved you, but forbidden you to partake
  of all the plants? How generous!
Why then do you make paradise
  your home, but are deprived of its delight?
  Therefore, how can you have *eternal life*?"

11

Deceived by these words, Eve answered him as follows:
  "You are in error and do not know what the Lord commanded.
God has given the whole of paradise as a table
to those he created, for their enjoyment;
but he prevented participation[9] in only one thing,
  which would become an obstacle to our life.
It is useful for us both
  and is able to teach us the knowledge of good and evil,
  for we have already received *as a possession eternal life.*"

[9]The Greek word (μετάληψιν) is an allusion to holy communion.

Ι Β

Ῥήματι οὖν θανατηφόρῳ   γλυκεῖαν ὁ ἐχθρὸς συγκατέμιξε γεῦσιν,
    σκεπτόμενος   καὶ λέγων ταῦτα   κατ᾽ ἰδίαν ὁ ἔχθιστος·
«Εἰ μὴ δόλῳ κεράσω τὸ βούλημα,
ἂν καταψηφίσωμαι   τοῦ Θεοῦ ἐν τοῖς λόγοις μου,
εὐθέως ὑποπτεύσει με   Εὔα ὡς μισόθεον,
    καὶ γενήσομαι πρὸς ταύτην   ἀπαράδεκτος·
οὐδὲ γὰρ οἶδα   τέως τὴν γνώμην
    ταύτης· ἐὰν ἰσχύσω   διαστρέψαι,   ἔστιν ὅτι στέργει με·
    ἐντέχνως οὖν προσέλθω   **τοῖς λαβοῦσι ζωὴν   τὴν αἰώνιον.**»

Ι Γ

Ὡς δὲ τοιαῦτα διενοήθη,   ὁ ὄφις πρὸς τὴν Εὔαν ἐφθέγξατο λέγων·
    «Συνήδομαι   τῇ ἀφθονίᾳ   τῆς τρυφῆς ἧς ἐλάβετε,
ἐπαινῶ τοῦ Θεοῦ τὴν ἀλήθειαν,
ὅτι οὐκ ἐψεύσατο   πρὸς ὑμᾶς διηγούμενος
ὡς μεγάλη ἡ δύναμις   τούτου τοῦ φυτοῦ ἐστι·
    τῶν καλῶν γὰρ καὶ τῶν φαύλων   γνῶσιν δίδωσι·
μόνος Θεὸς δὲ   διαγινώσκει
    διάκρισιν τὴν πάντων·   διὰ τοῦτο   τὴν τούτου μετάληψιν
    παρήγγειλε μὴ ἔχειν,   **ὃ παρέχει ζωὴν   τὴν αἰώνιον.**

Ι Δ

Μὴ γὰρ οὐκ οἶδα ὅτι τὴν κτίσιν   καλὴν ὁ Θεὸς ἀπειργάσατο
    πᾶσαν;
    Ὁ πάντα οὖν   καλὰ ποιήσας   πῶς φυτεῦσαι ἠνείχετο
παραδείσου εἰς μέσον τὸν θάνατον;
Οὐχ ὑπάρχει πρόσκομμα   τὸ φυτὸν τὸ τῆς γνώσεως·

12

Therefore, the enemy mixed a sweet taste with his death-bringing
    word, plotting, the bitterest enemy said these things in private:
"Unless I mingle my plan with trickery,
if I condemn God by my words,
Eve will at once suspect me of hating God,
    and I shall become unacceptable to her,
for until now, I do not know her will.
    If I manage to mislead, she might favor me.
    Therefore, let me approach with craft *those who have received
    eternal life.*"

13

After reflecting like this, the serpent addressed Eve saying:
    "I rejoice with you at the abundance of pleasure you have
    received;
I praise the truthfulness of God,
because he did not lie when he explained to you
how great is the power of this plant,
    for it gives knowledge of both good and evil.
But God alone has the power of discerning
    between all things. This is why he ordered you not to
    partake of it,[10] *for it gives eternal life.*"

14

"Do I not know that the creation that God has wrought is wholly
    good?[11] So how could the one who made all things good,
have allowed death to grow in the midst of paradise?
The plant of knowledge is not a stumbling block,

[10] Once again, Romanos employs the Greek word (μετάληψιν) as an allusion to holy communion.
[11] Genesis 1.31.

οὐδὲ γὰρ ἀποθνήσκετε   ἐὰν τοῦτο φάγητε·
    ὡς θεοὶ δὲ διὰ τούτου   νῦν γενήσεσθε
ὥσπερ ὁ κτίστης,   τοῦ διακρίνειν
    καλῶν καὶ φαύλων τρόπους·   διὰ τοῦτο   ἐν μέσῳ προτέθειται
    παντὸς τοῦ παραδείσου,   **ὥσπερ ἔχοντα ζωὴν τὴν   αἰώνιον.**»

ΙΕ

Αὕτη οὖν ἰδοῦσα τὸ δένδρον   ὡς ἔστιν εὐπρεπὲς καὶ ἐνάρετον
    Εὔα,
    ἐφλέγετο   καὶ πρὸς τὴν γεῦσιν   ταῖς ἐλπίσιν ἐπείγετο·
λογισμοῖς ἑαυτὴν συνεκίνησεν,
«Ὁ μηνύσας, λέγουσα,   οὐκ ἐχθρὸς τοῦ Θεοῦ ἐστιν;
Ποίαν ἔχθραν γὰρ κέκτηται   ὁ ὄφις πρὸς τὸν πλάσαντα;
    Τὸ φυτὸν δὲ καὶ τῇ θέᾳ   ἐστὶ πάγκαλον·
σπεύσω πρὸς βρῶσιν   θεοποιΐας
    καὶ ἀπολαύσω τούτου   οὗ τὴν θέαν   ὁρῶσα μαραίνομαι,
    καὶ δώσω τῷ ἀνδρί μου   **ἵνα σχῶμεν τὴν ἄφεσιν καὶ ζωὴν**   τὴν
    αἰώνιον.»

ΙΣΤ

Νῦν ἐδέξω θανατηφόρον,   ὦ τάλαινα Εὔα, καὶ ἔφαγες τούτου·
    τί τρέχεις οὖν   συναπολέσαι   καὶ τὸν ἄνδρα τὸν ἴδιον;
Ἀκριβῶς ἑαυτὴν κατεξέτασον,
εἰ ὃ προσεδόκησας   διὰ γεύσεως γέγονας,
εἰ θεὸς εἶ, ὡς ἤλπισας·   γνῶθι τοῦτο πρότερον,
    καὶ εἶθ᾽ οὕτως, πρὸς τὴν γεῦσιν   καὶ τὸν ἄνδρα σου,
γύναι, προτρέπου·   μὴ οὖν ποιήσῃς
    συγκτήτορα τὸν ἄνδρα   ἀπωλείας·   τί σπεύδεις νομίζουσα
    ὡς βρῶσίς σοι παρέσχεν   **ἡ τοῦ ξύλου τὴν ζωὴν**   τὴν **αἰώνιον**;

for you will not die if you eat it,
    but through it you will now become as gods,
like the Creator, able to discern
    ways of good and evil.[12] This is why it has been placed
    in the middle of the whole of paradise, *for it has eternal life.*"

15

Therefore, when she saw that the tree was beautiful and fair,[13]
    Eve was enflamed and yearned with hopes of tasting it.
With thoughts she stirred herself, saying,
"Can the one who revealed this be the enemy of God?
For what enmity can the serpent have toward the one who
    fashioned it? Moreover, the plant is most fair to look at.
I will hasten to the food that makes one divine,
    and I will enjoy this thing, at the sight of which I waste away,
    and I will give it to my husband, *that we may have forgiveness*
    and eternal life."

16

Now you have accepted what brings death, O wretched Eve, and
    eaten of it.
    So why do you run to destroy your own husband with yourself?
Examine yourself with care to see
if through tasting you have become what you expected,
if you are a god, as you hoped. Make sure of this first,
    and if it is so, invite your husband also,
O woman, to taste it. Do not then make
    your husband a co-owner of perdition. Why do you hasten,
    supposing that eating from *the tree* granted you *eternal life*?

---

[12]Genesis 3:5.
[13]Genesis 3:6.

ΙΖ

Ὅτε τῷ δένδρῳ ἐπιτερφθεῖσα   ἀπώλετο· οὐ γὰρ ἀπήλαυσεν Εὔα·
    ἐσπούδασε   καὶ ἐπεδίδου   καὶ Ἀδὰμ τοῦ καρποῦ αὐτοῦ,
καὶ ὡς μέγιστον δῶρον προσφέρουσα
οὕτως διεγίνετο·   πρὸς αὐτὸν δὲ ἐφθέγγετο·
«Θησαυρὸν παρετρέχομεν   μέχρι νῦν, ὦ σύζυγε,
    καὶ τρυφὴν τὴν μακαρίαν   ἐφοβούμεθα·
νῦν ἔγνων, ἄνερ,   καὶ ἐπειράθην
    ὡς ἄκαιρον δειλίαν   ἐκρατοῦμεν·   καὶ γὰρ ἐγὼ ἔφαγον
    καὶ ζῶσά σοι παρέστην   **καὶ ἀπέχω τὴν ζωὴν   τὴν αἰώνιον.**

ΙΗ

Ὑπάρχει μᾶλλον ὡς ἔχων πεῖραν   ὁ λόγος τοῦ μηνύσαντος
    βέβαιος ὄντως·
    φαγοῦσα γὰρ   οὐκ ἐνεκρώθην,   ὡς Θεὸς προηγόρευσεν,
ἀλλὰ ζῶσά σοι νῦν παραγέγονα,
καὶ σχηματισμός ἐστι   τοῦ Θεοῦ τὸ παράγγελμα·
εἰ γὰρ ἦν ἀληθέστατον,   ἄρτι συνεθρήνεις με
    ὡς θανοῦσαν καὶ κειμένην   πρὸς τὸν θάνατον.
Δέχου οὖν, ἄνερ, καὶ κατατρύφα·
    προσλάμβανε ἀξίαν   διὰ τούτου   τὴν θείαν καὶ ἄχραντον·
    θεὸς γενήσει ὥσπερ   **ὁ παρέχων τὴν ζωὴν   τὴν αἰώνιον.»**

ΙΘ

Ὁ μὲν οὖν ὄφις, ὡς φθάσας εἶπον,   ἐγγίσαι τῷ Ἀδὰμ οὐκ ἐθάρρησε
    τότε,
    φοβούμενος   μὴ διαμάρτῃ   τῆς ἐλπίδος ἧς ἔσπευδεν,
ἀλλὰ ἄλλος ἐφάνη δεινότερος
καὶ ὀφιωδέστερος   ὄφις τούτου τοῦ ὄφεως.
Ὃν γὰρ ὄφις οὐκ ἔδακεν,   αὕτη ἐθανάτωσε·
    κολακεύουσα γὰρ τότε   τὸν ἰὸν αὐτῆς

17

When Eve, bewitched by the tree, had perished, for she had taken
  no pleasure, she hurried and gave Adam of its fruit,
and as though offering the greatest gift
she acted thus: she said to him,
"O companion, until now, we have overlooked a treasure,
  and we have been afraid of a blessed delight.
Now I know, my husband, and have experienced that we have
  entertained a pointless cowardice, for I have eaten and I stand
  by you alive *and I receive eternal life.*"

18

The word of the one who initiated me is sure, and has proof,
  for having eaten I did not die, as God foretold,
but now I am with you still living,
and the order of God was a pretense.
For if it had been absolutely true, you would now be mourning me
  as dead and lying here in death.
Therefore, husband, take and enjoy,
  receive through this the divine and spotless dignity;
  a god you will become like *him who grants eternal life.*"

19

The serpent, as I have already said, had not dared to approach
  Adam,
  afraid that it might fail in the hope on which its heart was set,
but another one appeared, a serpent more fearsome
and more serpentine than this serpent.
For the one the serpent had not bitten, she put to death.
  For having enticed him, she then injects

τούτῳ ἐμβάλλει, καὶ ἑαυτήν τε
   κἀκεῖνον ἀπορρήσσει, καὶ σκευάζει ἀπάτη τῆς βρώσεως
   νεκροὺς ὀφιοπλήκτους **ἀπολέσαντας ζωὴν τὴν αἰώνιον.**

Κ

Ὑπὸ οὖν ταύτης πολιορκεῖται Ἀδὰμ τῆς ἀπάτης ὁ δείλαιος·
   μιᾷ μὲν γὰρ πληγῇ τιτρώσκει διὰ βρώσεως ἅπαντας·
διὰ τοῦτο δὲ οὕτως ὡς ἄτακτος
ἐν τοῖς πόνοις ἅπασιν ἐπὶ γῆς κατεβέβλητο·
πρὸς νηστείαν γὰρ σύμμετρον ὄντως καὶ ὠφέλιμον,
   μὴ μεθύειν ἀκρασίᾳ, οὐκ ἠνέσχετο·
χριστιανῶν δὲ πάντα τὰ γένη
   νηστείᾳ προσεθίζειν καὶ ἐρίζειν ἀγγέλοις ἐπείγονται,
   ἐλπίζοντα ἐντεῦθεν **προσλαμβάνειν τὴν ἄφεσιν καὶ ζωὴν τὴν
   αἰώνιον.**

ΚΑ

Μεγάλη ἐστὶν ἡ νηστεία πρὸς ἣν ὁ Ἀδὰμ ἐκεκλήρωτο πρώην·
   ἐν μόνοις γὰρ φυτοῖς ὑπῆρχεν ἡ τροφὴ τῷ γεννήτορι·
ἀκρατὴς δὲ καὶ οὗτος ἐγένετο.
Νῦν παντοδαπής ἐστι τῶν βρωμάτων ἀπόλαυσις,
τῶν ἰχθύων τὰ ἥδιστα, ὄρνεις καὶ τετράποδα,
   τῶν φυτῶν καὶ τῶν σπερμάτων τὰ ποικίλματα,
μαγγανεῖαι αἱ τῶν τρυφώντων,
   τῶν τραπεζῶν ἡ χάρις ἡ κινοῦσα ἡμᾶς πρὸς τὴν ὄρεξιν
   τὴν τῆς γαστριμαργίας, <**ἀφαιροῦσα δὲ ζωὴν τὴν αἰώνιον**>.

her venom, and breaks both herself
    and him; and the deception of the food renders them
    serpent-smitten[14] corpses *that have lost eternal life.*

20

So wretched Adam is besieged by this deception;
    for by a single blow through food he wounds all humankind.
Therefore, through lack of discipline
in pains of every kind he was thrown to the ground.
For he was unable through fasting, which is measured and useful,
    not to get drunk through intemperance;
while all the races of Christians
    strive by fasting to accustom themselves to and to rival angels,
    hoping thereby *to gain forgiveness and eternal life.*

21

Fasting is great, to which Adam had at first been destined;
    for our ancestor's nourishment consisted of plants alone;
but he became intemperate.
Now the enjoyment of foods is of every kind,
the sweetest of fish, birds, and quadrupeds,
    varieties of plants and seeds,
the artifices of those who fare sumptuously,
    the charm of tables, which stirs our appetite
    for gluttony, *depriving us of eternal life.*[15]

---

[14]The Greek word ὀφιόπληκτος is a *hapax legomenon*, a word occurring only once in Romanos' oeuvre and a word that is not found elsewhere in the Greek literature of antiquity and Byzantium.

[15]There is no refrain at the end of strophe 21 in the Patmos manuscript; this is a conjecture that appears in both of the critical editions.

ΚΒ

Νῦν ταῦτα λέγων, μὴ ἐρεθίσω   πολλοὺς πρὸς γυμνασίαν
    παμφάγον, ὦ φίλοι·
    μὴ δείξω δὲ   τοῦ πρωτοπλάστου   λιχνοτέρους ἐν βρώμασι·
τὸν γὰρ ζῆλον ἡμῶν, ὦ πιστότατοι,
περὶ τὴν ἐγκράτειαν   τὴν μεγίστην ἐκήρυξα·
λειτουργεῖν γὰρ ἐπείγεσθε,   τὴν νηστείαν στέργοντες,
    ἐτησίως νῦν δεκάτας   τῷ Θεῷ ἡμῶν,
ὥσπερ Ἑβραῖοι   ἐκ τῶν χρημάτων
    προσέφερον Κυρίῳ   τὰς δεκάτας,   τῷ τύπῳ σημαίνοντες
    τὴν μέλλουσαν νηστείαν   δι᾽ ἧς ἔχομεν ζωὴν   τὴν αἰώνιον.

ΚΓ

Ὁ ἀριθμὸς οὖν ἐν τῇ νηστείᾳ   δηλούσθω ὁ τῆς δεκατώσεως, φίλοι·
    ἑπτὰ μὲν γὰρ   αἱ ἑβδομάδες   τῆς νηστείας ὑπάρχουσιν·
αἱ δὲ πέντε ἡμέραι ὑπόψηφοι
ἐφ᾽ ἑκάστῃ δείκνυνται   ἑβδομάδι νηστεύσιμοι,
ὡς ὑπάρχειν τριάκοντα   πέντε ἃς νηστεύομεν,
    καὶ νυχθήμερον πρὸς τούτοις   τὸ τοῦ σαββάτου
τοῦ σωτηρίου   ἔχομεν πάθους·
    τριάκοντα ἓξ οὖν ἡμέραι πᾶσαι   καὶ ἥμισυ γίνονται,
    δεκάτωσις τοῦ ἔτους,   δι᾽ ἧς κτώμεθα ζωὴν   τὴν αἰώνιον.

ΚΔ

Σῶτερ τοῦ κόσμου, σὲ προσκυνοῦντες   λατρείαν λογικήν σοι
    προσφέρομεν ταύτην·
    φιλάνθρωπε   καὶ ἐλεῆμον,   σὺ τοὺς πάντας ἐλέησον·
καὶ ἐσθίοντες γὰρ καὶ νηστεύοντες,

2 2

O friends, saying this now, let me not provoke many to voracious
    exercise,
    nor teach you to be more gluttonous in foods than the
    first-formed.
O most faithful ones, I have proclaimed our zeal
for the greatest temperance.
For, loving fasting, you now hasten to offer your
    yearly tithe to our God,
just as the Jews from their goods
    offered tithes to the Lord,[16] signifying in a figure
    the fast to come, *through which we have eternal life.*

2 3

O friends, let the figure of the tithe be shown by the fast.
    For there are seven weeks of the fast;
in each week five days are shown
as allotted to fasting,
so, there are thirty-five days when we fast,
    and in addition to these we have the night and day of the
    Sabbath of the Savior's passion.
Therefore, the total days are thirty-six and a half,
    a tithe of the year,[17] *through which we gain eternal life.*

2 4

Savior of the world, as we adore you, we offer you this reasonable
    worship.[18]
    O Lover of humankind and merciful one, have mercy on all.
For both when we eat and when we fast,

[16]Genesis 14.20.
[17]On the notion of Lent as a tithe of the year and the number of days in Lent, see
Kallistos Ware and Mother Mary, *The Lenten Triodion* (Boston: Faber, 1978), 30–33.
[18]Romans 12.1.

πάντες σε δοξάζομεν   τὸν τοὺς πάντας ῥυόμενον
ἐκ τῆς πλάνης οὓς ἔπλασας·   σὺ γὰρ εἶ ὁ Θεὸς ἡμῶν,
    εἰ καὶ ἄνθρωπος ἐγένου,   ὡς ἠθέλησας,
ἐκ τῆς παρθένου   καὶ παναγίας
    Μαρίας τῆς ἀχράντου   Θεοτόκου·   διὸ σοὶ προσπίπτομεν·
    πρεσβείαις τῆς μητρός σου,   **δὸς τοῖς δούλοις σου ζωὴν   τὴν
    αἰώνιον.**

we all give you glory,[19] you who deliver from error
all whom you fashioned. For you are our God,
   though you also became human, as you willed,
from the Virgin and all-holy
   Mary the immaculate Theotokos; therefore, we fall before you.
   Through the entreaties of your mother, *give your servants
   eternal life.*

---

[19] 1 Corinthians 10.31.

Γ
Εἰς τὸν ἄσωτον υἱόν

Τῇ κυριακῇ τῆς β´ ἑβδομάδος τῶν νηστειῶν, κοντάκιον
κατανυκτικὸν εἰς τὸν ἄσωτον υἱόν, φέρον ἀκροστιχίδα
τήνδε· δέησις καὶ ταύτη ἡ τοῦ Ῥωμανοῦ
πλ. δ´, πρός· Τὸν πρὸ ἡλίου ἥλιον.

Προοίμιον ι

Τὸν ἄσωτον ἐζήλωσα   ταῖς ἀτόποις μου πράξεσι,
    καὶ ὡς ἐκεῖνος προσπίπτω σοι   καὶ ζητῶ τὴν ἄφεσιν, Κύριε·
    διὸ μὴ παρίδῃς με,   ὁ τῶν αἰώνων δεσπότης καὶ κύριος.

Προοίμιον ιι

Τῆς μυστικῆς σου   τραπέζης, ἀθάνατε,
    τὸν ἀσωτίᾳ   φθαρέντα ἀξίωσον,
    καὶ τὴν πρώτην καταστολὴν   τῆς χάριτός
    ἣν παθῶν ταῖς κηλῖσιν   ὁ τάλας ἐμόλυνα
    οἰκτιρμοῖς ἀνεφίκτοις   καὶ πάλιν μοι δώρησαι
    ὁ τῶν αἰώνων   δεσπότης καὶ κύριος.

Α

Δεῖπνον κατίδωμεν ἡμεῖς   εὐτρεπισθὲν ἐξαισίως
    τῷ πρώην μὲν ἀσώτῳ,   σωφρονήσαντι δὲ ὅμως·
    πατὴρ γὰρ ὁ τούτου   ἢ μᾶλλον πάντων ἀνθρώπων

3
On the Prodigal Son

On Sunday of the second week of Lent, a kontakion of
compunction on the prodigal son,[1] bearing the following
acrostic: another entreaty by Romanos.
Fourth plagal [mode], according to: "The sun before the sun."

PRELUDE 1

O Lord, I have emulated the prodigal son by my senseless deeds
and, like him, I fall down before you and I seek forgiveness.
Therefore, do not despise me, *Master and Lord of the ages.*

PRELUDE 2

O Immortal One, deem me, who have been corrupted by
prodigality, worthy of your mystical table.[2]
And the first garment of grace,
which I have defiled, wretch that I am, by the stains of the
passions, in your unattainable compassions give me once again,
Master and Lord of the ages.

1

Let us behold a supper marvellously spread
for the former prodigal now become temperate.
For his father, or rather the Father of all humankind,

---

[1]Luke 15.11–32.
[2]The "mystical table" is an allusion to the Eucharist.

μετανοοῦντα τοῦτον δέχεται ὡς φιλάνθρωπος,
    τῇ δὲ μετανοίᾳ χαίρων τῇ τούτου
    λέγει πρὸς τοὺς δούλους· «Σπεύσατε τὸ δεῖπνον ἡμῖν
        ποιῆσαι τὸ πανάγιον.
Σπεύσατε, θύσατε πάντως τὸν μόσχον
    ὅνπερ ἐγέννησε παρθένος δάμαλις,
    ὅτι ὁ υἱός μου ἀπώλετο πρώην
    καὶ νῦν εὑρέθη· ἀλλ' εὐφρανθῶμεν·
νεκρὸς ἦν καὶ ἀνέζησεν
    ὃν ἔλαβον ἐν τοῖς σπλάγχνοις μου,
    ὁ τῶν αἰώνων δεσπότης καὶ κύριος.»

Β

Ἔνθεν σπουδάσωμεν νυνὶ καὶ μετάσχωμεν τοῦ δείπνου,
    ἐὰν ἀξιωθῶμεν τῷ πατρὶ συνευφρανθῆναι·
    συνεστιαθῶμεν τῷ βασιλεῖ τῶν ἀγγέλων·
ἄρτους παρέχει τοὺς διδοῦντας μακαριότητα,
    πόμα δὲ δωρεῖται ἅγιον αἷμα
    πρόξενον ἀφθάρτου καὶ ἀτελευτήτου ζωῆς,
        παρίστανται δὲ ἄγγελοι.
Ἴδωμεν πρῶτος μὲν πῶς ἀνεκλίθη
    αὐτὸς ὁ κύριος ὁ προτρεψάμενος·
    εὐθὺς πατριάρχαι, χοροὶ ἀποστόλων
    καὶ οἱ προφῆται μετὰ μαρτύρων·
πλησίον δὲ ἀνέκλινε
    τὸν ἄσωτον υἱὸν αὐτοῦ
    ὁ τῶν αἰώνων δεσπότης καὶ κύριος.

Γ

Ἡ δὲ ἑστία τίς ἐστι μάθωμεν πρῶτον τοῦ δείπνου
    ἐκ τῶν εὐαγγελίων, ἵνα καὶ ἐπευφρανθῶμεν·
    τῆς οὖν τοῦ ἀσώτου παραβολῆς μνημονεύσω·

receives him repentant, in his love for humankind,
    rejoicing at his repentance,
    says to the servants, "Hurry, make ready for us
                the all-holy supper.
Hurry, above all sacrifice the calf
    to which a virgin heifer gave birth,
    because my son was lost before
    and has now been found. But let us celebrate;
he was dead and has returned to life,
    he whom I have taken in my heart,
    the Master and Lord of the ages."

2

From here let us now hasten and share in the supper;
    if we have been deemed worthy to rejoice with the Father.
    Let us banquet with the king of the angels.
He provides bread that gives blessedness.
    As drink, he gives holy blood,
    a source of life without corruption and without end,
                while angels stand and wait.
Let us see how the first to take his place
    was the Lord himself who urges us,
    then at once patriarchs, choirs of apostles,
    and the prophets with the martyrs.
He makes his prodigal son
    take his place near him,
    the Master and Lord of the ages.

3

What is the banquet? Let us first learn of the supper
    from the Gospels, so that we too may celebrate.
    I will therefore recall the parable of the Prodigal.

οὗτος γὰρ πρώην ἐγυμνώθη πάσης τῆς χάριτος,
    πᾶσαν τὴν οὐσίαν καταναλώσας,
    καὶ πρὸς τὸν πατέρα τρέχει σὺν πολλοῖς ὀδυρμοῖς
        βοῶν· «Πάτερ, ἡμάρτηκα».
Εἶδεν οὖν, ἔσπευσε πάντα ὁ βλέπων
    καὶ ὑπαπήντησε καὶ κατεφίλησε
    τὸν τράχηλον τούτου τοῦ ἐπιστραφέντος·
    θεὸς γὰρ ἔστι μετανοούντων·
ἠλέησεν ὡς εὔσπλαγχνος
    τὸν πταίσαντα υἱὸν αὐτοῦ
    ὁ τῶν αἰώνων δεσπότης καὶ κύριος.

Δ

Σωτὴρ ὁ πάντων κατιδὼν ῥερυπωμένην ἐσθῆτα
    τότε ἠμφιεσμένον τὸν υἱὸν κατεσπλαγχνίσθη·
    εὐθὺς οὖν τοῖς δούλοις τοῖς ὑπουργοῦσιν ἐβόα·
«Δότε συντόμως τὴν στολὴν τὴν πρώτην τῷ τέκνῳ μου
    ἣν ἡ κολυμβήθρα πᾶσιν ὑφαίνει,
    ἣν κατασκευάζει χάρις ἡ τοῦ πνεύματός μου,
        καὶ σπεύσαντες ἐνδύσατε·
μέμνησθε πῶς αὐτὸν ἐνδεδυμένον
    ἐχθρὸς ἀπέδυσε καὶ ἐδειγμάτισε
    τοῖς δαίμοσι πᾶσι, βαλλόμενος φθόνῳ
    τὸν βασιλέα τῆς γῆς ἁπάσης,
δι᾽ ὃν τὸν κόσμον ἅπαντα
    ἐκόσμησα ὃν παρήγαγον,
    ὁ τῶν αἰώνων δεσπότης καὶ κύριος.

Ε

Ἴδον αὐτὸν καὶ παριδεῖν οὐ στέγω τὸν γυμνωθέντα·
    οὐ φέρω βλέπειν οὕτως τὴν εἰκόνα μου τὴν θείαν·
    ἐμὴ γὰρ αἰσχύνη τὸ ὄνειδος τοῦ παιδός μου·

For he was formerly stripped bare of every grace,
   having squandered all his substance,
   and he runs to his Father with many lamentations
             crying out, "Father, I have sinned."
Therefore, the one who sees all things saw, hastened,
   and met him and kissed him,
   flung his arms round the neck of the one who had returned,
   for he is the God of those who repent.
In his compassion he had mercy
   on his son who had fallen, he
   the Master and Lord of the ages.

4

The Savior of all, seeing his son then clothed
   in filthy apparel, was filled with compassion,
   and, therefore, he cried at once to the servants who were serving:
"Quickly, give my child the first robe,
   which the baptismal font weaves for all,
   which the grace of my Spirit prepares,
            and hasten and clothe him.
Remember how when he was clothed
   the enemy stripped him and made him a spectacle
   for all the demons, as he attacked with envy
   the king of the whole earth,
for whose sake I arrayed the whole world
   that I had created, I
   the Master and Lord of the ages."

5

"I saw him and I cannot allow myself to overlook his nakedness;
   I cannot bear to see my divine image like this.
   For the disgrace of my child is my shame;

ἰδίαν δόξαν   τὴν τοῦ τέκνου δόξαν ἡγήσομαι.
    Σπεύσατε οὖν, δοῦλοι   καὶ λειτουργοί μου,
    ἀνακαλλωπίσαι   ἅπαντα τὰ μέλη αὐτοῦ·
                        εἰσὶ γάρ μοι ἐράσμια.
Κρίνω γὰρ   ἄτοπον   τοῦτον ὁρᾶσθαι
    ἢ ἀπρονόητον   ἢ ἀκαλλώπιστον
    τὸν ἐν μετανοίᾳ   ἐμοὶ προσδραμόντα
    καὶ τῆς συγγνώμης   ἀξιωθέντα·
στολὴν τοῦτον ἐνδύσατε
    τῆς χάριτος,   ὡς προσέταξα
    ὁ τῶν αἰώνων   δεσπότης καὶ κύριος.

ΣΤ

Στήλη αἰδέσιμος ἵνα   ἐστὶ τῇ κτίσει ὁ παῖς μου,
    τὴν χεῖρα δακτυλίῳ   καλλωπίσατε τὴν τούτου·
    ἀρραβὼν γὰρ ἔστι   τριάδος τῆς ἀχωρίστου,
ἵνα φρουρεῖται   ὑπὸ ταύτης, ὡς προσδραμὼν αὐτῇ,
    ἵνα τὴν σφραγῖδα   ταύτην προφέρων
    φαίνεται μακρόθεν   ὅτι υἱός μου ἐστὶν
                        τοῦ πάντων βασιλεύοντος·
γένηται   γνώριμος   τοῖς ἐναντίοις
    καὶ φοβερώτατος   φανῇ τοῖς δαίμοσι
    καὶ τῷ διαβόλῳ   τῷ ὑπερηφάνῳ,
    ἵνα μηκέτι   αὐτῷ ἐγγίζῃ·
ὁρῶν γὰρ τὴν σφραγῖδά μου
    οὐχ ἵσταται   ἥνπερ δίδωμι,
    ὁ τῶν αἰώνων   δεσπότης καὶ κύριος.

Ζ

Καὶ οὐδὲ πόδας τοὺς αὐτοῦ   ἀνασφαλίστους ἐάσω·
    οὐ θέλω οὐδὲ τούτους   γεγυμνῶσθαι τῆς προνοίας·
    ὑποδήσατε οὖν   συντόμως τὸν γυμνωθέντα,

I will consider the glory of my child my own glory.
    Hurry then, my servants and ministers,[3]
     to make all his limbs beautiful once again,
                for they are objects of my love.
For I judge it improper to see
    unprovided for, or unadorned,
     the one who has run to me in repentance
     and been found worthy of forgiveness.
Clothe him with the robe
    of grace, as I have commanded, I
    the Master and Lord of the ages."

6

"So that my child may be a venerable monument for creation,
    adorn his hand with a ring.
     It is a pledge of the undivided Trinity,
to guard him since he has had recourse to it,
    so that when he displays this seal
     it may appear from afar that he is my son, the son
              of the ruler of all.
May he become well-known to his enemies
    and appear most fearful to the demons
    and the arrogant devil,
    so that he may no longer approach him.
For he will not stand his ground on seeing my seal,
    which I give, I
    the Master and Lord of the ages."

7

"Nor will I allow his feet to be unprotected.
    I do not wish that they should be stripped of my care.
    Quickly put shoes on the one who was stripped naked,

[3]Psalm 103.4.

μὴ πάλιν εὕρῃ   ὁ πανοῦργος ὄφις καὶ δόλιος
    πτέρναν τοῦ παιδός μου   γεγυμνωμένην
    καὶ ἐπιβουλεύσῃ   διὰ τῆς κακίας αὐτοῦ
                        τῷ πράῳ ὁ παμπόνηρος.
Δύναμιν   δίδωμι   τῷ υἱῷ μου,
    ἵν᾽ ὡς ἀδύνατον   πατῇ τὸν δράκοντα,
    ἵνα ἐπιβαίνῃ   μετὰ παρρησίας
    ἐπὶ ἀσπίδα   καὶ βασιλίσκον,
καὶ ἐπὶ τὸν παράδεισον
    πορεύεται   ὃν ἐφύτευσα,
    ὁ τῶν αἰώνων   δεσπότης καὶ κύριος.

Η

Ἀλλ᾽ ὑπὲρ πταίσαντος λοιπὸν   θύσατε νῦν, καθὼς εἶπον,
    τὸν μόσχον τὸν παρθένον   τὸν υἱὸν τὸν τῆς παρθένου,
    τὸν μὴ δαμασθέντα   ζυγῷ τῷ τῆς ἁμαρτίας,
τὸν προθυμίᾳ   πρὸς τοὺς ἕλκοντας πορευόμενον·
    οὐ γὰρ στασιάζει   πρὸς τὴν θυσίαν,
    ἀλλὰ τὸν αὐχένα   κλίνει ἑκουσίως αὐτοῖς
                        τοῖς θύειν ἐπισπεύδουσιν.
Ἕλκετε,   θύσατε   τὸν ζωοδότην
    τὸν καὶ θυόμενον   καὶ μὴ νεκρούμενον,
    τὸν ζωοποιοῦντα   πάντας τοὺς ἐν ᾅδῃ,
    ἵνα φαγόντες   ἐπευφρανθῶμεν·
νεκρὸς γὰρ ἦν, ὡς πρόειπον,
    καὶ ἔζησεν   ὃν ἐλέησα
    ὁ τῶν αἰώνων   δεσπότης καὶ κύριος.

Θ

Ἱερεῖς, δοῦλοί μου πιστοί,   θύσατε τοῦτον τὸν μόσχον
    καὶ δότε πᾶσι τρώγειν   τοῖς τοῦ δείπνου μου ἀξίοις
    τὸν ἄσπιλον μόσχον,   τὸν καθαρὸν κατὰ πάντα,

so that the crafty and deceitful serpent may not find once again the
    heel of my child stripped naked; nor may the
      thoroughly depraved one through his wickedness lay a trap
                      for the meek one.
I give power to my son,
    so that he may trample on the dragon as powerless,
    may march with confidence
    upon asp and basilisk,[4]
and walk in paradise
    which I planted, I
    the Master and Lord of the ages."

8

"But now, as I said, sacrifice the virgin calf for the one who
    has stumbled, sacrifice the Son of the Virgin,
    he who has never been tamed by the yoke of sin;
with eagerness he goes ahead of those who drag him,
    for he does not revolt against the sacrifice,
    but willingly bows his neck
                  to those who hasten to sacrifice him.
Drag in, sacrifice, the giver of life,
    who is sacrificed and not put to death,
    who gives life to those in hell,
    so that, as we eat, we may celebrate,
for he was dead, as I said before, and has come to life,
    the one on whom I have had mercy, I
    the Master and Lord of the ages."

9

"O priests, my faithful servants, sacrifice this calf
    and, to all who are worthy of my supper, give to eat
    the spotless calf, pure in every way,

[4]Psalm 90.13.

τὸν σιτευθέντα   ἐξ ἀσπόρου γῆς ἦσπερ ἔπλασε·
    δότε δὲ πρὸς τούτοις   τίμιον πόμα,
    αἷμά τε καὶ ὕδωρ   τὸ ἐκ τῆς πλευρᾶς τῆς αὐτοῦ
                    πηγάζον τοῖς πιστεύουσι.
Πάντες οὖν   πάντοτε   φάγετε τοῦτον·
    κἂν γὰρ μελίζεται,   ἀλλ’ οὐ μερίζεται,
    οὐδὲ διαιρεῖται,   οὐδὲ δαπανᾶται,
    ἀλλ’ εἰς αἰῶνας   χορτάζει πάντας·
εἰς ἔδεσμα γὰρ πρόκειται
    πανάγιον   ὁ φιλάνθρωπος,
    ὁ τῶν αἰώνων   δεσπότης καὶ κύριος.»

I

Τῶν κεκλημένων πᾶς λοιπὸν   ὁ θίασος ὡς ἐδείπνει
    καὶ πάντες εὐφρανθέντες   ἐμελῴδουν θεῖον ὕμνον·
    ὁ πατὴρ μὲν πρῶτος   κατήρξατο τῶν παρόντων,
«Γεύσασθε, λέγων,   καὶ ἴδετε ὅτι Χριστός εἰμι».
    Εἶτα μετὰ ταῦτα   ὁ ψαλμολόγος
    κρούων τὴν κιθάραν   κράζει ἡδυτάτῃ φωνῇ·
                    «Σπουδαίως προσαγάγετε
θύματα   ἄχραντα,   εὐλογημένα,
    πρὸς τὸ πανάγιον θυσιαστήριον·
    ἀνοίσατε μόσχον   μετ’ εὐχαριστίας.»
Καὶ μετ’ αὐτὸν δὲ   βοᾷ ὁ Παῦλος·
«Τὸ πάσχα τὸ ἡμέτερον
    ἐτύθη νῦν   Ἰησοῦς Χριστός,
    ὁ τῶν αἰώνων   δεσπότης καὶ κύριος.»

fattened from the unsown earth that he fashioned.
　　Give to them a precious drink,
　　blood and water that springs from his side[5]
　　　　　　　　for those who believe.
Eat this then, all of you always,
　　for though it is parted, it is not divided,
　　not separated, not consumed,
　　but satisfies all unto the ages,[6]
for he offers himself as all-holy food,
　　the Lover of humankind,
　　the Master and Lord of the ages."

10

As the whole company of the invited were supping
　　and as all were celebrating, they sang a divine hymn.
　　The Father, first of those present, began.
"Taste" he said "and see that I am Christ."[7]
　　Then after this the psalmist,
　　striking the lyre, cries with sweetest voice,
　　　　　　　　"Quickly bring
sacrifices, pure, blessed,
　　to the all-holy altar.
　　Bring a calf with thanksgiving."[8]
　　And after him Paul cried out,
"Our Passover has
　　now been sacrificed, Jesus Christ,[9]
　　the Master and Lord of the ages."

---

[5]John 19.34.

[6]This is possibly the earliest witness in Byzantium to the wording of the fraction prayer, which today in the Divine Liturgy reads as follows: "Broken and distributed is the Lamb of God: broken, yet not divided; ever eaten, yet never consumed, but sanctifying those who partake thereof." (Μελίζεται καὶ διαμερίζεται ὁ Ἀμνός τοῦ Θεοῦ, ὁ μελιζόμενος, καὶ μὴ διαιρούμενος, ὁ πάντοτε ἐσθιόμενος, καὶ μηδέποτε δαπανώμενος, ἀλλὰ τοὺς μετέχοντας ἁγιάζων).

[7]Cf. Psalm 33.9.

[8]Psalm 50.21.

[9]1 Corinthians 5.7.

ΙΑ

Ἄγγελοι εἴδοσαν αὐτοὺς   οἱ ὑπουργοῦντες τῷ δείπνῳ
   οὕτως εὐφραινομένους   καὶ συντόνως μελῳδοῦντας,
   καὶ ζηλοῦσι τούτους   καὶ ἤρξαντο ὑμνῳδίας·
τίς δὲ ὁ ὕμνος   ἐπακούσωμεν, εἰ δοκεῖ ὑμῖν·
   «Ἅγιος εἶ, πάτερ,   ὁ εὐδοκήσας
   τοῦ σφαγιασθῆναι   ὑπὲρ τῶν ἀνθρώπων νυνὶ
                  τὸν μόσχον τὸν ἀκήρατον·
ἅγιος   ἔστι δὲ   καὶ ὁ υἱός σου
   ἑκὼν θυόμενος   ὡς μόσχος ἄσπιλος,
   ὃς καὶ ἁγιάζει   τοὺς βαπτιζομένους
   ἐν τῇ δυνάμει   τῆς κολυμβήθρας·
τὸ πνεῦμα πάλιν ἅγιον
   ὃ δίδωσι   τοῖς πιστεύουσιν
   ὁ τῶν αἰώνων   δεσπότης καὶ κύριος.»

ΙΒ

Υἱὸς ὁ πρῶτος παντελῶς   ταῦτα ἠγνόει, διότι
   ἐτύγχανεν ἐκεῖνος   εἰς ἀγρὸν πεπορευμένος·
   ἀλλὰ ὑποστρέψας   ἀκούει τῆς συμφωνίας
καὶ παῖδα ἕνα   μεταπέμπεται καὶ πυνθάνεται·
   «Τί ἂν εἴη τοῦτο;   λέγε συντόμως·
   καὶ γὰρ μυστικός μοι   ἦχος εἰς τὰ ὦτα κτυπεῖ
                  μεγάλης πανηγύρεως·
λέγε μοι   τί ἐστι   τοῦτο τὸ δρᾶμα·
   τίς τὰ προσήκοντα   ἐμοὶ μυστήρια
   καὶ πάντα τὸν πλοῦτον   τῆς θείας θυσίας
   ἐμοῦ ἀπόντος   μερίζει ἄλλοις;
Μὴ ἄρα πάλιν δίδωσι
   χαρίσματα   ὁ γεννήσας με
   ὁ τῶν αἰώνων   δεσπότης καὶ κύριος;»

11

The angels who were serving at the supper saw them
　　celebrating like this and singing with one accord,
　　and they emulated them and began their song of praise.
What was the hymn? Let us hear, if you will:
　　"Holy are you, Father, who have been well-pleased
　　for the spotless calf to be now
　　　　　　　　　slaughtered for humankind.
Holy also is your Son,
　　willingly sacrificed as an unblemished calf,
　　and who hallows those who are baptized
　　by the power of the font.
Again, holy is the Holy Spirit,
　　whom he gives to those who believe,[10] he
　　the Master and Lord of the ages."

12

The first son was ignorant of all these things, because
　　he happened to have gone to the fields.
　　But, having returned, he hears the music,
summons a servant, and asks him:
　　"So what is all this? Tell me at once;
　　for a mysterious sound of a great festival
　　　　　　　　　strikes my ears.
Tell me what is this event?
　　The mysteries that belong to me
　　and all the wealth of the divine sacrifice,
　　who, in my absence, is sharing them with others?
Can he be bestowing once again
　　gifts of grace, he who begot me,
　　the Master and Lord of the ages?"

[10]The hymn the angels sing in this strophe is based on the Trisagion: "Holy God, Holy Mighty, Holy Immortal, have mercy on us."

ΙΓ

Τότε ὁ παῖς ἐρωτηθεὶς εἶπεν πρὸς τοῦτον σπουδαίως
ὅτι «Ὁ ἀδελφός σου παρεγένετο ὁ νέος·
ηὐφράνθη δὲ τοῦτον ἀπολαβὼν ὁ πατήρ σου,
καὶ ἐπειδήπερ ἐρρωμένον τοῦτον ἐδέξατο,
ἔθυσε τὸν μόσχον τὸν σιτευθέντα
καὶ ἐπὶ τὸ δεῖπνον τοῦτο προετρέψατο νῦν
                    τοὺς φίλους καὶ γνωστοὺς αὐτοῦ.»
Ταῦτα οὖν ἅπαντα οὗτος ἀκούσας
    εὐθὺς ἐξίστατο καὶ οὐκ ἐβούλετο
    τῷ δείπνῳ παρεῖναι τῷ τῆς εὐωχίας,
    ὡς ὠργισμένος τοῖς γινομένοις,
εἰπών· «Οὐκ εἰσελεύσομαι,
    οὐκ ὄψομαι ἃ ἐποίησεν
    ὁ τῶν αἰώνων δεσπότης καὶ κύριος.»

ΙΔ

Ἡμῖν ὑπογραμμὸν Χριστὸς τῆς ἑαυτοῦ εὐσπλαγχνίας
    διδάσκει διὰ τούτου καὶ ἀμέτρου συμπαθείας
    τῆς καὶ τοὺς δικαίους πρὸς φθόνον ἐρεθιζούσης.
Δεῦτε οὖν, γνῶμεν πῶς παρακαλῶν αὐτὸν ἵσταται
    οὗτος ὁ γεννήσας τοὺς ἀμφοτέρους,
    οὗτος ὁ τῶν ὅλων πρύτανις καὶ κτίστης Θεός,
                    ὁ θέλων πάντας σῴζεσθαι·
ἄφατος, ἄφραστος τοῖς σῳζομένοις
    ἡ εὐσπλαγχνία σου ἐστί, φιλάνθρωπε·
    τοὺς μὲν γὰρ δικαίους ἀεὶ θεραπεύεις,
    ἁμαρτωλοὺς δὲ ἀνακαλεῖσαι·
τὸν δίκαιον ἐφύλαξας,
    τὸν ἄλλον δὲ περιέσωσας,
    ὁ τῶν αἰώνων δεσπότης καὶ κύριος.

13

Then the servant who had been questioned said to him earnestly,
    "Your young brother has arrived.
    On receiving him, your Father rejoiced,
and, as he has recovered him in good health,
    he has sacrificed the fatted calf
    and now summoned his friends and
                    acquaintances to the supper."
On hearing all this,
    he was immediately astonished and was not willing
    to take part in the supper of festivity.
    Angered by what was happening
he said, "I will not go in,
    I will not look on what he has done,
    the Master and Lord of the ages."

14

Christ teaches us, through this, an example
    of his own compassion and measureless sympathy,
    which rouses even the just to indignation.
Come then, let us learn how he stood and entreated him,
    he who begot them both,
he who is governor and creator of all things, the God who wishes
                all to be saved.[11]
Ineffable, inexpressible is your compassion
    for those who are saved, O Lover of humankind,
    for you always heal the righteous,
    while you call sinners back again.
The righteous you kept safe,
    while the other you saved, you
    the Master and Lord of the ages.

[11] 1 Timothy 2.4.

ΙΕ

Ἤγειρε πεσόντα υἱὸν   δοὺς δεξιὰν ὁ οἰκτίρμων,
    τὸν ἄλλον δὲ ὁμοίως   ὑπεστήρισεν ἑστῶτα·
    τὸν κείμενον κάτω   ἀνέστησε συμπαθήσας,
τὸν δὲ ἑστῶτα   πεσεῖν ὅλως οὐ συνεχώρησε·
    τὸν μὲν ἐν πενίᾳ   ὄντα πλουτίζει,
    τὸν δὲ ἐν τῷ πλούτῳ   γενέσθαι οὐκ εἴασε πτωχόν,
                    ἀλλ᾽ ἔσωσε τοὺς ἅπαντας.
Δεῦτε οὖν,   μάθωμεν   τί τῷ πατρὶ μὲν
    ὁ παῖς ἐφθέγγετο   καὶ οὐκ ἐβούλετο
    τῷ δείπνῳ παρεῖναι   τῷ εὐτρεπισθέντι,
    ὡς ὠργισμένος   τοῖς γινομένοις·
αὐτὸς δὲ ὁ πατὴρ αὐτοῦ
    πῶς ἵστατο   δυσωπῶν αὐτόν,
    ὁ τῶν αἰώνων   δεσπότης καὶ κύριος.

ΙΣΤ

Ῥήματα ἔφη τῷ πατρὶ   ὁ υἱὸς ἀγανακτήσας·
    «Τοσοῦτον χρόνον ἔχω   τῇ βουλήσει σου δουλεύων
    καὶ ταῖς ἐντολαῖς σου   ἀεὶ ὑπηρετησάμην,
καὶ οὐδεμίαν   ἐντολήν σου ὅλως παρέτρωσα·
    οἶδας, κἂν μὴ λέγω,   ὡς ἀληθεύω,
    καὶ ὑπὲρ τῶν πόνων   τούτων οὐ παρέσχες ἐμοὶ
                    ὡς τέκνῳ σου κἂν ἔριφον·
πάντοτε   θλίβομαι   ἐν ἐρημίαις
    καὶ ὑστερούμενος   καὶ κακουχούμενος
    ἐν καύσωσι πλείστοις   καὶ ἐν τοῖς χειμῶσιν,
    ἵνα ἀρέσω   τῇ σῇ δυνάμει,
καὶ ὅλως ἐπιστρέψαντα
    τὸν ἄσωτον   προετίμησας,
    ὁ τῶν αἰώνων   δεσπότης καὶ κύριος.

15

Offering his right hand, the compassionate one raised the fallen
    son. Likewise, he supported the other who was standing. The
    one who was laid low he raised up in his compassion,
while he would in no way allow the one who stood to fall.
    The one in poverty he enriches;
        the one in wealth he would not allow to become poor,
                but saved them all.
Come then, let us learn what the youth said
    to his Father, and how he refused
    to be present at the supper that had been prepared,
    for he was angered at what was happening,
and how his Father
    stood imploring him,
    he who is Master and Lord of the ages.

16

The indignant son spoke these words to his Father,
    "For so long a time I have been a slave of your will
    and have always served your commandments,
and not a single commandment of yours have I transgressed at all.
    You know, even if I do not say it, that what I say is true.
    And, for these toils, you have not allowed me,
                as your child, even a kid.
I am oppressed unceasingly in deserts
    and deprive myself and am tormented
    by the fiercest heats and by the winters,
    that I may satisfy your power.
And yet, the prodigal who returned, you honored
    above all others, you
    the Master and Lord of the ages."

ΙΖ

Ὡς εἶδες δὲ τὸν ὕϊὸν   τοῦτον τὸν καταφαγόντα
    τὸν πλοῦτόν σου σὺν πόρναις,   εὐθὺς ἔσφαξας τὸν μόσχον·
    ἐχρῆν γάρ, ὡς οἶμαι,   κἂν μέμψασθαι διὰ λόγων
καὶ διελέγξαι,   ἀποστρέψαι δὲ καὶ τὸ πρόσωπον·
    ἀλλὰ παραχρῆμα   τοῦτον ἐδέξω,
    καὶ κατηλέησας,   πρῶτον συνεπλάκης αὐτῷ,
                στολῇ δὲ κατεκόσμησας·
ἔντιμον   ἔδειξας   τῷ δακτυλίῳ
    καὶ περιέσφιγξας   τοῖς ὑποδήμασιν·
    ἐποίησας δεῖπνον   πρὸς τὴν εὐωχίαν
    καὶ προετρέψω   τοὺς φίλους πάντας·
τιμὰς τοιαύτας ἔδωκας
    τῷ πταίσαντι,   ἐπιστρέψαντι,
    ὁ τῶν αἰώνων   δεσπότης καὶ κύριος.»

ΙΗ

Μόνον δὲ ταῦτα ὁ πατὴρ   ἤκουσε παρὰ τοῦ τέκνου,
    εὐθέως ἀπεκρίθη   σὺν πραότητι πρὸς τοῦτον·
    «Κλῖνόν σου τὰ ὦτα   καὶ ἄκουσον τοῦ πατρός σου.
Σὺ μετ᾽ ἐμοῦ εἶ,   οὐκ ἀπέστης γάρ μου οὐδέποτε·
    σὺ τῆς ἐκκλησίας   οὐκ ἐχωρίσθης·
    σύ μοι συντυγχάνεις   πάντοτε παρὼν σὺν ἐμοί,
                σὺν πᾶσι τοῖς ἀγγέλοις μου.
Οὗτος δὲ   ἤλυθε   κατησχυμμένος,
    γυμνὸς καὶ ἄμορφος,   βοῶν· Ἐλέησον·
    ἡμάρτηκα, πάτερ,   καὶ καθικετεύω
    ὁ πλημμελήσας   ἐνώπιόν σου·
ὡς μίσθιόν με πρόσδεξαι
    καὶ θρέψον με   ὡς φιλάνθρωπος,
    ὁ τῶν αἰώνων   δεσπότης καὶ κύριος.ʼ

17

"When you saw this son who has devoured
    your wealth with harlots, you slaughtered the calf at once.
    You should, in my opinion, have at least reproached him
in words and rebuked him and, at the same time,
    turned away your face. But you instantly received him,
    and you had compassion on him. First you embraced him, then
                decked him out in a robe.
You showed him honor with a ring.
    You shod him with sandals.
    You made a supper for celebration
    and invited all his friends.
Such are the honors you gave
    the offender who returned, you
    the Master and Lord of the ages."

18

No sooner had the Father heard these words from his child
    than he answered him with meekness,
    "Incline your ears and listen to your Father.[12]
You are with me, for you have never left me.
    You have not been separated from the Church.
    Your place is always with me,
               with all my angels.
But he has come covered with shame,
    Naked and ugly, crying out, 'Have mercy.
    I have sinned, Father, and I implore,
    I who have offended before you,
accept me as a hired servant
    and, as Lover of humankind, nourish me, you
    the Master and Lord of the ages.'"

[12]Psalm 16.6.

ΙΘ

Ἀδελφὸς ἔκραξεν ὁ σός· ˙Σῶσόν με, ἅγιε πάτερ΄.
   Τί εἶχον οὖν ποιῆσαι τοῦ κλαυθμοῦ τούτου ἀκούων;
   Πῶς δὲ ἐδυνάμην μὴ ἐλεῆσαι καὶ σῶσαι
τὸν ὑϊόν μου τὸν θρηνοῦντα καὶ ὀδυρόμενον;
   Σὲ κριτὴν αἱροῦμαι τὸν ἐγκαλοῦντα·
   δίκασόν μοι, τέκνον, ὁ καταμεμφόμενός μοι,
           καὶ γίνου διαγνώμων μοι.
Χαίρω γὰρ πάντοτε φιλανθρωπίᾳ·
   πῶς οὖν ἀπάνθρωπος γενέσθαι ἴσχυον;
   Ὅν ἔπλασα πρώην πῶς μὴ ἐλεήσω
   καὶ οἰκτειρήσω μετανοοῦντα;
Τὰ σπλάγχνα μου ἐγέννησαν
   τὸ τέκνον μου ὃ ἐλέησα
   ὁ τῶν αἰώνων δεσπότης καὶ κύριος.

Κ

Νόει ἃ λέγω σοι, υἱέ· τὰ ἐμὰ πάντα σὰ ἔστι,
   κἀκείνῳ ἐβουλήθην παρασχεῖν τῶν ἀγαθῶν μου·
   ἀμείωτος ἔστιν ἣν ἔχεις περιουσίαν·
οὐ γὰρ ἐκ ταύτης λαβὼν δέδωκα τῷ συγγόνῳ σου·
   ἐκ τῶν θησαυρῶν μου τούτῳ παρέσχον.
   Εἷς εἰμι τῶν δύο κτίστης καὶ πατὴρ ἀγαθός,
           φιλάνθρωπος καὶ εὔσπλαγχνος·
σὲ τιμῶ, τέκνον μου, ὡς προαιρέσει
   ἀεί με στέρξαντα καὶ θεραπεύσαντα,
   κἀκείνῳ συμπάσχω διὰ τὸ σπουδάσαι
   τῇ μετανοίᾳ προσκαρτερῆσαι·
εὐφραίνεσθαι οὖν ἔδει σε
   σὺν ἅπασιν οἷσπερ κέκληκα,
   ὁ τῶν αἰώνων δεσπότης καὶ κύριος.

19

"Your brother cried, 'Save me, holy Father.'
    What should I have done as I heard his lamentation?
    How could I not have mercy and save
my son as he grieved and wept?
    You, the prosecutor, I appoint as judge.
    Sentence me, my child, as you blame me,
                and become my arbitrator.
For I always rejoice in loving humankind.
    How then could I become inhuman?
    How should I not have mercy on the one I fashioned of old
    and take pity on him when he repents?
It was my womb that begot my child
    on whom I have had mercy, I
    the Master and Lord of the ages."

20

"Understand what I say, my son. All that is mine is yours,[13]
    and to him I wanted to grant some of my goods.
    The property that you have is not any less,
for I did not take from it to give to your brother;
    I provided for him from my own treasures.
    Of you both, I am Creator and loving Father,
                Lover of humankind and compassionate.
I honor you, my child, for by choice
    you have always loved me and served me,
    and to him I show compassion because of his earnestness
    and persistence in repentance.
You should be celebrating then
    with all whom I invited, I
    the Master and Lord of the ages."

[13]Luke 15.31; John 17.10.

ΚΑ

Ὅθεν σὺν ἄπασιν, υἱέ,   τοῖς εἰς τὸ δεῖπνον κληθεῖσιν
 εὐφραίνου καὶ μελῴδει   μετὰ πάντων τῶν ἀγγέλων·
 ὁ γὰρ ἀδελφός σου   ἀπώλετο καὶ εὑρέθη·
οὗτος νεκρὸς ἦν   καὶ ἀπροσδοκήτως ἀνέζησε.»
 Ταῦτα οὖν ἀκούσας   οὗτος ἐπείσθη
 καὶ ἠγαλλιᾶτο   μετὰ τοῦ συγγόνου αὐτοῦ,
   καὶ ψάλλων ταῦτα ἔλεγεν·
«Ἅπαντες   κράξατε   μετ' εὐφημίας,
 ὅτι μακάριοι   ὧνπερ ἀφίεται
 πᾶσα ἁμαρτία,   καὶ ἡ ἀνομία
 ἐπεκαλύφθη   καὶ ἐξηλείφθη.
Σὲ εὐλογῶ, φιλάνθρωπε,
 ὃς ἔσωσας   καὶ τὸν σύγγονον,
 ὁ τῶν αἰώνων   δεσπότης καὶ κύριος.»

ΚΒ

Υἱὲ καὶ Λόγε τοῦ Θεοῦ,   δημιουργὲ τῶν ἁπάντων,
 αἰτοῦντες δυσωποῦμεν   οἱ ἀνάξιοί σου δοῦλοι·
 ἐλέησον πάντας   τοὺς σὲ ἐπικαλουμένους·
ἡμαρτηκότας   ὡς τὸν ἄσωτον περιποίησαι·
 πρόσδεξαι καὶ σῶσον   δι' εὐσπλαγχνίας
 τοὺς ἐν μετανοίᾳ   τρέχοντας πρὸς σέ, βασιλεῦ,
   κραυγάζοντας· «Ἡμάρτομεν.»
Δὸς ἡμῖν   δάκρυα,   ὥσπερ τῇ πόρνῃ,
 καὶ τὴν συγχώρησιν   ὧνπερ ἡμάρτομεν,
 καὶ ὡς τὸν τελώνην   οἰκτείρησον πάντας
 ταῖς ἱκεσίαις   τῆς Θεοτόκου,
μετόχους τε τοῦ δείπνου σου
 ἀνάδειξον   ὡς τὸν ἄσωτον,
 ὁ τῶν αἰώνων   δεσπότης καὶ κύριος.

2 1

"Therefore, my son, with all those who have been invited to the
    supper, celebrate and sing with all the angels,
    for your brother was lost and has been found.
He was dead and, beyond expectation, has returned to life."
    When he heard these words, he was persuaded
    and shared the gladness with his brother.
                And he began to sing and say,
"All of you shout with praise,
    that blessed are they whose every
    sin is forgiven, and whose iniquity
    has been covered and wiped away.[14]
I bless you, Lover of humankind,
    who have saved my brother also, you
    the Master and Lord of the ages."

2 2

O Son and Logos of God, Creator of all things,
    we your unworthy servants ask and implore you,
    have mercy on all who call upon you.
As you did the prodigal son, spare those who have sinned.
    Accept and save through compassion
    those who in repentance run to you, O King,
                crying, "We have sinned."
Give us tears, as you did the harlot,
    and forgiveness for the sins we have committed.
    And, as you did the publican, take pity on us all,
    through the intercessions of the Theotokos.
Make us partakers of your supper,
    as you did the prodigal son, you
    the Master and Lord of the ages.

[14]Psalm 31.1.

Δ

[No title in the Patmos manuscript]

Τῇ τετράδι τῆς μεσονηστίμου, κοντάκιον σταυρώσιμον,
φέρον ἀκροστιχίδα τήνδε· τοῦ ταπεινοῦ Ῥωμανοῦ
ἦχος βαρύς, ἰδιόμελον.

Προοίμιον I

Οὐκέτι φλογίνη   ῥομφαία φυλάττει   τὴν πύλην τῆς Ἐδέμ·
    αὐτῇ γὰρ ἐπῆλθε,   παράδοξος δέσις,   τὸ ξύλον τοῦ σταυροῦ·
θανάτου τὸ κέντρον   καὶ ᾅδου τὸ νῖκος   ἐνήλωτο·
    ἐπέστης δέ, σωτήρ μου,   βοῶν τοῖς ἐν ᾅδῃ·   «Εἰσάγεσθε
πάλιν εἰς τὸν παράδεισον.»

Προοίμιον II

Ὡς ἀληθῶς λύτρον ἀντὶ πολλῶν   προσηλωθεὶς τῷ τύπῳ τοῦ
    σταυροῦ,
    Χριστὲ ὁ Θεὸς ἡμῶν,   ἐξηγοράσω ἡμᾶς·
τῷ τιμίῳ γὰρ   φιλανθρώπως αἵματι
    τὰς ψυχὰς ἡμῶν   ἐκ θανάτου ἥρπασας,
    συνεισενέγκας ἡμᾶς   **πάλιν εἰς τὸν παράδεισον.**

Προοίμιον III

Τὰ οὐράνια καὶ τὰ ἐπίγεια   συγχαίρουσι δικαίως τῷ Ἀδὰμ
    ὅτι κέκληται   **πάλιν εἰς τὸν παράδεισον.**

On the Victory of the Cross

On Wednesday of mid-Lent, a crucifixion kontakion,
bearing the following acrostic: by the humble Romanos.
Grave mode, Idiomelon

PRELUDE 1

A fiery sword no longer guards the gate of Eden,[1]
    for a strange bond came upon it: the wood of the Cross.
The sting of Death and the victory of Hades were nailed to it.
    But you appeared, my Savior, crying to those in hell:
    "Be brought back *again to paradise.*"

PRELUDE 2

Having been nailed to the form of the Cross as truly a ransom
    for many,[2]
    you redeemed us, Christ our God,
for by your precious blood in love for humankind
    you snatched our souls from death,
    you brought us back with you *again to paradise.*

PRELUDE 3

Heavenly and earthly things rightly rejoice with Adam,
    for he has been called *again to paradise.*

[1]Genesis 3.24.
[2]Matthew 20.28.

Α

Τρεῖς σταυροὺς ἐπήξατο   ἐν Γολγοθᾶ ὁ Πιλᾶτος,
  δύο τοῖς ληστεύσασι   καὶ ἕνα τῷ ζωοδότῃ·
  ὃν εἶδεν ὁ Ἅιδης   καὶ εἶπε τοῖς κάτω·
«Ὦ λειτουργοί μου   καὶ δυνάμεις μου,
  τίς ὁ ἐμπήξας   ἧλον τῇ καρδίᾳ μου;
Ξυλίνη με λόγχη ἐκέντησεν ἄφνω καὶ διαρρήσσομαι·
  τὰ ἔνδον πονῶ,   τὴν κοιλίαν μου ἀλγῶ·
  τὰ αἰσθητήριά μου·   μαιμάσσει τὸ πνεῦμά μου,
καὶ ἀναγκάζομαι   ἐξερεύξασθαι
  τὸν Ἀδὰμ καὶ τοὺς Ἀδὰμ   ξύλῳ δοθέντας μοι·
  ξύλον τούτους εἰσάγει   **πάλιν εἰς τὸν παράδεισον.**»

Β

Ὅτε τούτων ἤκουσεν   ὁ δολιόβουλος ὄφις,
  ἔδραμε συρόμενος   καὶ κράζει· «Ἅιδη, τί ἔχεις;
  Τί μάτην στενάζεις;   Τί λόγους προσφέρεις;
Τοῦτο τὸ ξύλον   ὅπερ ἔφριξας
  τῷ ἐκ Μαρίας   ἄνω ἐτεκτόνευσα·
ἐγὼ Ἰουδαίοις ὑπέδειξα τοῦτο   πρὸς τὸ συμφέρον ἡμῖν·
  ἔστι γὰρ σταυρὸς   ᾧ προσήλωσαν Χριστόν·
  ξύλῳ γὰρ θέλω ἀνελεῖν   τὸν Ἀδὰμ τὸν δεύτερον.
Μὴ οὖν ταράξῃ σε,   οὐχ ἁρπάσει σε·
  μεῖνον ἔχων οὓς κρατεῖς;   ὧν γὰρ δεσπόζομεν
  οὐδὲ εἷς ἀποφεύγει   **πάλιν εἰς τὸν παράδεισον.**»

Γ

«Ὕπαγε, ἀνάνηψον,   Βελίαρ, κράζει ὁ Ἅιδης·
  δράμε, ἀποκάλυψον   τοὺς ὀφθαλμούς σου, καὶ ἴδε
  τοῦ ξύλου τὴν ῥίζαν   ἐντὸς τῆς ψυχῆς μου·

1

Pilate fixed three crosses on Golgotha,
    two for the robbers and one for the giver of life,
    whom Hades saw, and he said to those below,
"O my ministers and powers,
    who has fixed a nail in my heart?
A wooden lance has suddenly pierced me and I am being torn
    apart. My insides are in pain, my belly in agony,
    my senses make my spirit tremble,[3]
and I am compelled to disgorge
    Adam and Adam's race. Given me by a tree,
    a tree is bringing them back *again to paradise*."

2

When he heard this, the cunning serpent
    ran crawling and cried, "What is it, Hades?
    Why do you groan for no reason? What words do you offer?
This tree, at which you tremble,
    I carpentered up there for Mary's child.
I intimated it to the Jews for our advantage,
    for it is a cross, to which I have nailed Christ,
    wishing by a tree to do away with the second Adam.
Therefore, do not upset yourself. It will not plunder you.
    Keep hold of those you have. Of those whom we rule,
    not one escapes *again to paradise*."

3

"Away with you, come to your senses, Beliar," cried Hades.
    "Run, open your eyes, and see
    the root of the tree inside my soul.

[3]Jeremiah 4.19.

κάτω κατῆλθεν   εἰς τὰ βάθη μου
    ἵν᾽ ἀνασπάσῃ   τὸν Ἀδὰμ ὡς σίδηρον.
Τὴν τούτου εἰκόνα ποτὲ Ἐλισσαῖος   προεζωγράφησεν
    ἐκ τοῦ ποταμοῦ   τὴν ἀξίνην ἀνελών·
    τῷ ἐλαφρῷ τὸ βαρὺ   ὁ προφήτης εἵλκυσε,
προοιμιάζων σοι   καὶ διδάσκων σε
    ὅτι ξύλῳ ὁ Ἀδὰμ   μέλλει ἀνάγεσθαι
    ἀπὸ ταλαιπωρίας   **πάλιν εἰς τὸν παράδεισον.**»

Δ

«Τίς τοιαύτην ἔννοιαν   ὑπέθετό σοι, ὦ Ἅιδη;
    Πόθεν ἐδειλίασας   ἐν φόβῳ οὗ οὐκ ἦν φόβος,
    ἐκ ξύλου ἀτίμου,   ξηροῦ καὶ ἀκάρπου,
τοῦ γενομένου   πρὸς ἀναίρεσιν
    τῶν κακουργούντων   καὶ χαιρόντων αἵμασι;
Πιλᾶτος γὰρ τοῦτο ἐφεῦρε, πεισθείς μου   τοῖς συμβουλεύμασι,
    καὶ τρέμεις αὐτό,   καὶ ἡγεῖσαι δυνατόν;
    Τὸ τιμωρὸν πανταχοῦ   παρὰ σοῦ σωτήριον;
Τίς ὁ πλανήσας σε;   Τίς δ᾽ ὁ πείσας σε
    ὅτι ξύλῳ ὁ πεσὼν   ξύλῳ ἀνίσταται
    καὶ καλεῖται οἰκῆσαι   **πάλιν εἰς τὸν παράδεισον;**»

Ε

«Ἄφρων ἄφνω γέγονας,   ὁ πρώην φρόνιμος ὄφις·
    πᾶσα ἡ σοφία σου   διὰ σταυροῦ κατεπόθη
    καὶ ἐν τῇ παγίδι   τῇ σῇ ἐζωγρεύθης·
ἆρον τὸ ὄμμα   καὶ θεώρησον
    ὅτι εἰς βόθρον   ὃν εἰργάσω ἔπεσας.

It has gone down to my depths,
     to draw up Adam like iron.
Elisha of old painted its image in prophecy
     when he drew the axe head from the river.[4]
     With a light object the prophet dragged a heavy,
warning you, and teaching you
     that, by a tree, Adam is to be brought up
     from wretchedness *again to paradise*."

4

"Who gave you such an idea then, Hades? From where
     now this cowardly fear, where once there was no fear,[5]
     of a worthless tree, dry and barren,
ready for the removal of malefactors
     and those who welcome bloodshed?
For Pilate discovered it, persuaded by my counsels,
     and do you fear it, and reckon it powerful?
     With you, the universal executioner, will it prove salvation?
Who has misled you? Who has persuaded you that he who fell by a
     tree is being raised by a tree, and, so that
     he may dwell there, is being called *again to paradise*?"

5

"You have suddenly lost your senses, you of old the cunning
     serpent.[6] All your wisdom has been swallowed up through the
     Cross,[7] and you have been caught in your own snare.
Lift up your eyes and see that you have fallen
     into the pit that you created.

---

[4] 4 Reigns (2 Kings) 6.5–7.
[5] Psalm 13.5.
[6] Genesis 3.1.
[7] Psalm 106.27.

Ἰδοὺ γὰρ τὸ ξύλον ἐκεῖνο, ὃ λέγεις   ξηρὸν καὶ ἄκαρπον,
    βλαστάνει καρπὸν   οὗ γευσάμενος λῃστὴς
    τῶν ἀγαθῶν τῆς Ἐδὲμ   κληρονόμος γέγονεν·
ὑπὲρ τὴν ῥάβδον γὰρ   τὴν ἐξάξασαν
    ἐξ Αἰγύπτου τὸν λαὸν   τοῦτο ἐνήργησε·
    τὸν Ἀδὰμ γὰρ εἰσάγει   **πάλιν εἰς τὸν παράδεισον.**»

ΣΤ

«Παῦσαι, Ἅιδη ἄθλιε,   δειλῶν ἀπόσχου ῥημάτων·
    οὗτοι γὰρ οἱ λόγοι σου   τοὺς λογισμούς σου δηλοῦσι·
    σταυρὸν ἐφοβήθης   καὶ τὸν σταυρωθέντα,
ὧν οὐδὲ εἷς με   παρεσάλευσε·
    τῆς γὰρ βουλῆς μου   δράματα ὑπάρχουσιν·
θελήσω δὲ πάλιν καὶ μνῆμα ἀνοίξω   καὶ ἐντυμβεύσω Χριστόν,
    ἵν’ οὕτως ἔχῃς   τὴν δειλίαν σου διπλῆν,
    ἀπὸ τοῦ τάφου αὐτοῦ   ὡς ἐκ τοῦ σταυροῦ αὐτοῦ·
ἐγὼ δὲ βλέπων σε   ἐγγελάσω σε·
    θαπτομένου γὰρ Χριστοῦ,   ἔρχομαι λέγων σοι·
    Ἦον Ἀδὰμ τίς εἰσάγει   **πάλιν εἰς τὸν παράδεισον;**»

Ζ

Ἔκραξε δὲ ἄθροον   πρὸς τὸν διάβολον Ἅιδης·
    πῆρος τῷ μὴ βλέποντι,   τυφλὸς τυφλῷ λέγει· «Βλέψον,
    ἐν σκότει πορεύει,   ψηλάφα μὴ πέσῃς·
νόει ὃ λέγω,   βαρυκάρδιε,
    ὅτι ὃ πράττεις   ἔσβεσε τὸν ἥλιον.
Αὐτὸ γὰρ τὸ ξύλον εἰς ὃ ἐγκαυχᾶσαι   τὸ πᾶν ἐσάλευσεν,
    ἐκλόνησε γῆν,   ἐκάλυψεν οὐρανόν,
    ἔρρηξε πέτρας ὁμοῦ   καὶ τὸ καταπέτασμα,
καὶ τοὺς ἐν μνήμασιν   ἐξανέστησε,
    καὶ βοῶσιν οἱ νεκροί·   Ἅιδη, κατάλαβε·
    ὁ Ἀδὰμ γὰρ ὑπάγει   **πάλιν εἰς τὸν παράδεισον.**»

Behold that tree, which you call dry and barren,
    bears fruit; a robber tasted it
    and has become heir to the good things of Eden.
For it has outdone the rod
    that led the people out of Egypt,[8]
    for it is bringing Adam back *again to paradise.*"

6

"Wretched Hades, cease this cowardly talk;
    these words of yours reveal your thoughts.
    Were you afraid of a cross and of the crucified one?
Not one of your words has shaken me,
    for these deeds are part of my plan;
I would again both open a tomb and entomb Christ,
    so you may enjoy your cowardice double,
    from his tomb as well as from his Cross.
But when I see you, I shall mock you.
    For, when Christ is buried I shall come to you and say,
    'Who now is bringing Adam back *again to paradise*?'"

7

Suddenly Hades began to call out to the devil,
    the eyeless to the sightless, the blind to the blind: "Look,
    you are walking in darkness, feel around, lest you fall.
Consider what I tell you, slow of heart,
    because what you are doing has quenched the sun.[9]
The tree that you boast of has shaken the universe,
    has convulsed the earth, hidden the sky,
    rent the rocks together with the veil,
and raised up those in the tombs.[10]
    And the dead are shouting, 'Hades, understand,
    for Adam is hurrying back *again to paradise.*'"

[8]Exodus 14.16.
[9]Matthew 27.45.
[10]Matthew 27.51–53.

Η

«Ἴσχυσε πτοῆσαί σε   τοῦ Ναζωραίου τὸ ξύλον;»
  ἔφη ὁ διάβολος   πρὸς τὸν ὀλέθριον Ἅιδην.
«Σταυρῷ ἐνεκρώθης   ὁ πάντας νεκρώσας;
Ὅλως εἰ ξύλον   σε ἐπτόησε,
  ἔδει σε φρῖξαι   τοῦ Ἀμὰν τὴν σταύρωσιν
κἀκεῖνον τὸν πάσσαλον ᾧπερ ἀνεῖλε   τὸν Σισάρα Ἰαὴλ
  καὶ πέντε σταυροὺς   οἷς προσήλωσέ ποτε
  τοὺς τυραννοῦντας αὐτῷ   Ἰησοῦς ὁ τοῦ Ναυῆ·
περισσοτέρως δὲ   πτοησάτω σε
  τὸ φυτὸν τὸ ἐν Ἐδέμ,   ὅτι ἐξήγαγε
  τὸν Ἀδὰμ καὶ οὐκ εἰσάγει   **πάλιν εἰς τὸν παράδεισον.**»

Θ

«Νῦν καιρὸς ἀνοῖξαί σοι   τὰς ἀκοάς σου, Βελίαρ·
  νῦν ἡ ὥρα δείξει σοι   τὴν τοῦ σταυροῦ δυναστείαν
  καὶ τοῦ σταυρωθέντος   πολλὴν ἐξουσίαν.
Σοὶ μὲν μωρία   ὁ σταυρός ἐστι,
  πάσῃ δὲ κτίσει   θρόνος τεθεώρηται
ἐν ᾧ Ἰησοῦς ἡλωμένος, καθάπερ   ἐπικαθήμενος,
  ἀκούει λῃστοῦ   ἐκβοῶντος πρὸς αὐτόν·
  ‘Κύριε, μνήσθητί μου   ἐν τῇ βασιλείᾳ σου.’
Καὶ ἀποκρίνεται   ὡς ἐκ βήματος
  ὅτι· ‘Σήμερον, πτωχέ , συμβασιλεύσεις μοι·
  μετ’ ἐμοῦ γὰρ εἰσέρχῃ   **πάλιν εἰς τὸν παράδεισον.**’»

8

"Has the Nazarene's tree been strong enough to scare you?" said
    the devil to Hades the destroyer,
    "Have you been slain by a cross, you who slay all?
Truly if a tree has scared you,
    the crucifixion of Haman should have frightened you,[11]
and that stake with which Jael did away with Sisara,[12]
    and the five crosses to which Jesus of Navi
    once fixed those who tyrannized him.[13]
More than all, let the plant in Eden
    scare you, because it led out
    Adam, yet does not lead him back *again to paradise*."

9

"Now is the moment for you to open your ears, Beliar.
    Now the hour will show you the power of the Cross
    and the great authority of the Crucified.
For you, the Cross is folly,[14]
    but for all creation, it is seen as a throne,
on which, as though seated, Jesus is nailed,
    and hears the robber crying to him,
    'Lord, remember me in your kingdom,'
and answers as from a tribune,
    'Today, poor beggar, you will reign with me.
    For, with me, you will go in *again to paradise*.'"[15]

[11]Esther 7.10.
[12]Judges 4.21–22.
[13]Joshua 10.26.
[14]1 Corinthians 1.18.
[15]Luke 23.42–43.

I

Ὅτε τούτων ἤκουσεν   ὁ πολυμήχανος δράκων,
    ὥρμησε τρυχόμενος   καὶ ἅπερ ἤκουσεν εἶδε,
    λῃστὴν μαρτυροῦντα   Χριστῷ μαρτυροῦντι·
ὅθεν πρὸς ταῦτα   ἐκπληττόμενος,
    τύπτει τὸ στῆθος   καὶ διαλογίζεται·
«Λῃστῇ ὁμιλεῖ, καὶ τοῖς κατηγοροῦσιν   οὐκ ἀποκρίνεται·
    Πιλᾶτόν ποτε   οὐδὲ λόγου ἀξιῶν,
    νῦν προσφωνεῖ τῷ φονεῖ   λέγων· ʽΔεῦρο τρύφησον.᾿
Τί τὸ γενόμενον;   Τί ἑώρακεν
    ἐν σταυρῷ πρὸς τὸν λῃστήν,   ἔργα ἢ ῥήματα,
    διὰ ποῖον λαμβάνει   **τοῦτον εἰς τὸν παράδεισον;**»

I A

Ὕψωσε δὲ δεύτερον   φωνὴν ἰδίαν ὁ δαίμων
    κράζων· «Ἅιδη, δέξαι με,   πρὸς σὲ ἡ ἀποστροφή μου·
    τὰ σὰ γὰρ ὑπέστην   τοῖς σοῖς μὴ πιστεύσας.
Εἶδον τὸ ξύλον   ὅπερ ἔφριξας
    πεφοινιγμένον   αἵματι καὶ ὕδατι
καὶ ἔφριξα, οὐκ ἐκ τοῦ αἵματος λέγω,   ἀλλ᾽ ἐκ τοῦ ὕδατος·
    τὸ μὲν γὰρ δηλοῖ   τὴν σφαγὴν τοῦ Ἰησοῦ,
    τὸ δὲ τὴν τούτου ζωήν·   ἡ ζωὴ γὰρ ἔβλυσεν
ἐκ τῆς πλευρᾶς αὐτοῦ·   οὐχ ὁ πρῶτος γάρ,
    ἀλλ᾽ ὁ δεύτερος Ἀδὰμ   Εὔαν ἐβλάστησε,
    τὴν μητέρα τῶν ζώντων,   **πάλιν εἰς τὸν παράδεισον.**»

10

When he heard this, the resourceful[16] dragon
    began to wilt, and what he heard he saw,
    a robber witnessing to Christ crucified.
And so, astounded at this,
    he strikes his breast and argues,
"He speaks to a robber, yet does not answer his accusers?
    To Pilate he never deigned so much as a word;
    now he addresses a murderer, saying, 'Come, live in pleasure.'
What is this? Who has seen,
    where the robber on the Cross is concerned, words or deeds
    by means of which he is taking *this man to paradise*?"

11

A second time the demon raised the same cry,
    calling out, "Receive me, Hades. My recourse is to you;
    I submit to your views, I who did not believe them.
I saw the tree at which you shuddered,
    crimsoned with blood and water.[17]
And I shuddered, not, I tell you, at the blood, but at the water.
    For the former shows the slaughter of Jesus,
    but the latter, his life, because life has gushed
from his side. For it was not the first
    but the second Adam who carried Eve,
    the mother of all the living,[18] *again to paradise*."

---

[16]The Greek word πολυμήχανος was an epithet of Odysseus, a protagonist of many devices.
[17]John 19.34.
[18]Genesis 3.20.

ΙΒ

Ῥήμασι χρησάμενος   τοιούτοις ὁ παμπανοῦργος
    μόλις ὡμολόγησε   συμπεπτωκέναι τῷ Ἅιδῃ·
    ἀμέλει γοῦν ἅμα   θρηνοῦσι τὸ πτῶμα·
«Τί, φησί, τοῦτο   ὃ ὑπέστημεν;
    Πόθεν τῷ ξύλῳ   τούτῳ ἐνεπέσαμεν;
Εἰς ὄλεθρον ἡμῶν ἡ τούτου φυτεία   ἐνερριζώθη τῇ γῇ·
    στελέχη πικρὰ   ἐγκεντρίσαντες αὐτῷ,
    τὸν ἐν αὐτῷ γλυκασμὸν   οὐ μετεποιήσαμεν.
—Οἴμοι συνόμιλε.   —Οἴμοι σύντροφε·
    ὡς ἐπέσαμεν ὁμοῦ,   οὕτω πενθήσωμεν·
    ὁ Ἀδὰμ γὰρ ὑπάγει   **πάλιν εἰς τὸν παράδεισον.**

ΙΓ

Ὦ πῶς οὐκ ἐμνήσθημεν   τῶν τύπων τούτου τοῦ ξύλου·
    πάλαι γὰρ ἐδείχθησαν   πολυμερῶς, πολυτρόπως,
    ἐν τοῖς σῳζομένοις   καὶ ἀπολλυμένοις.
Ξύλῳ ὁ Νῶε   διεσῴζετο,
    κόσμος δὲ ὅλος   ἀπειθήσας ὤλετο·
Μωσῆς δι᾽ αὐτοῦ ἐδοξάσθη, τὴν ῥάβδον   καθάπερ σκῆπτρον
    λαβών, ἡ Αἴγυπτος δὲ   ταῖς πληγαῖς ταῖς ἐξ αὐτοῦ
    ὥσπερ βαθείαις πηγαῖς   ἐμπεσοῦσα πνίγεται.
Ἃ νῦν γὰρ ἔπραξε,   πάλαι ἔδειξεν
    ἐν εἰκόνι ὁ σταυρός·   τί οὖν οὐ κλαίομεν;
    Ὁ Ἀδὰμ γὰρ ὑπάγει   **πάλιν εἰς τὸν παράδεισον.**

ΙΔ

«Μεῖνον, Ἅιδη ἄθλιε»,   στενάζων ἔφη ὁ δαίμων.
    «Σίγησον, καρτέρησον,   ἐπίθες στόματι χεῖραν·
    φωνῆς γὰρ ἀκούω   χαρὰν μηνυούσης·

12

With such words the wholly wicked one
  barely admitted that he had fallen together with Hades.
  And so together they bewail their fall:
"To what," says the devil, "have we brought ourselves?
  How have we fallen by this tree?
For our destruction its planting was rooted in the earth.
  We grafted to it bitter shoots.
  We did not transform the sweetness in it."
"Alas, my comrade." "Alas, my companion."
  "As we have fallen together, so let us grieve,
  for Adam is going back *again to paradise.*

13

"O how did we not remember the types of this tree!
  For of old they were shown forth in many and varied ways in
  the saved and in the lost.[19]
By a tree, Noah was saved,
  but the whole world, unbelieving, was destroyed.
Moses was glorified through one when he took a staff as a scepter,
  but Egypt, with the plagues that came from it,
  was drowned as though fallen into deep wells.
What it has now done, the Cross showed forth
  of old in image. Why then are we weeping?
  For Adam is going *again to paradise.*"

14

"Wait, wretched Hades," said the demon with a groan,
  "Quiet, be patient, lay hand on mouth,
  for I hear a voice revealing joy.

---

[19]Hebrews 1.1; 1 Corinthians 1.18.

ἦχός μοι ἦλθεν   ἀγαθάγγελος,
    κτύπος ῥημάτων   ὥσπερ φύλλων τοῦ σταυροῦ·
Χριστὸς γάρ, ὡς μέλλων νεκροῦσθαι, ἐβόα   τὸ ʽΠάτερ, ἄφες
    αὐτοῖς·᾽ ἀλλ᾽ ἔθλιψέ με   τὸ μετέπειτα εἰπὼν
    ὅτι ʽΟὐκ οἴδασι τί   ποιοῦσιν οἱ ἄνομοι.᾽
Ἡμεῖς δὲ οἴδαμεν   ὅτι κύριος
    δόξης ἐστὶν ὁ παθὼν   καὶ ὅτι βούλεται
    τὸν Ἀδὰμ εἰσενέγκαι   **πάλιν εἰς τὸν παράδεισον.**»

ΙΕ

«Ἄρα ὅπερ ἔδειξε   τῷ Μωϋσῇ ὁ δεσπότης
    ξύλον ὃ ἐγλύκανε   ποτὲ τὸ ὕδωρ εἰς Μέρραν,
    ἐδίδαξε τί ἦν   καὶ τίνος ἡ ῥίζα;
τότε οὐκ εἶπεν·   οὐ γὰρ ἤθελε·
    νῦν δὲ τοῖς πᾶσι   τοῦτο ἐφανέρωσεν.
Ἰδοὺ γὰρ τὰ πάντα ἡδύνθη, ἡμεῖς δὲ   παρεπικράνθημεν·
    ἐκ ῥίζης ἡμῶν   ἀνεβλάστησε σταυρὸς
    ὃς ἐνεβλήθη τῇ γῇ   καὶ γλυκεῖα γέγονεν·
ἡ ἀνατείλασα   τὰς ἀκάνθας πρὶν
    νῦν ὡς ἄμπελος Σωρὴχ   κλάδους ἐξέτεινε
    μεταφυτευομένους   **πάλιν εἰς τὸν παράδεισον.**»

ΙΣΤ

«Νῦν οὖν, Ἅιδη, στέναξον,   καὶ συμφωνῶ σοι τοῖς γόοις·
    κλαύσωμεν θεώμενοι   ὃ ἐφυτεύσαμεν δένδρον
    μεταβεβλημένον   εἰς ἅγιον πρέμνον,
οὗ ὑποκάτω   κατεσκήνωσαν
    καὶ ἐπὶ κλάδοις   τούτου ἐννοσσεύουσι

A sound has reached me bringing good tidings,
    a rustle of words like the leaves of the Cross.
For Christ at the point of death cried out, 'Father, forgive them.'
    But he grieved me when he then said
    that the lawless know not what they do.'[20]
But we know that it is the Lord
    of glory[21] who is suffering and that he wishes
    to bring Adam back *again to paradise*."

15

"Did the Master, by the tree he showed to Moses,
    the very one that once sweetened the water at Mara,[22]
    teach what it was and what was its root?
Then, he did not say, for it was not his will.
    But now he has made it clear to all.
For behold, all things have been made pleasant, but we have been
    embittered.[23] From our root, a Cross has blossomed, which was
    cast into the earth, which became sweet.
The root, which formerly bred thorns,
    now like a Sorech vine[24] has spread branches,
    which are transplanted *again to paradise*."

16

"Now therefore, Hades, groan and I will harmonize with your
    wails. Let us lament as we see the tree that we planted
    transformed into a holy trunk,
beneath which have sheltered
    and will nest in its branches[25]

[20]Luke 23.34.
[21]1 Corinthians 2.8.
[22]Exodus 15.2325.
[23]Isaiah 14.9.
[24]Isaiah 5.2.
[25]Psalm 79.912.

ληισταί, φονευταὶ καὶ τελῶναι καὶ πόρναι,   ἵνα τρυγήσωσι
      καρπὸν γλυκασμοῦ   ἀπὸ τοῦ δῆθεν ξηροῦ·
      ὡς γὰρ φυτῷ τῆς ζωῆς   τῷ σταυρῷ προσπλέκονται,
ἐπερειδόμενοι   καὶ νηχόμενοι
      ἐκπερῶσι δι' αὐτοῦ   καὶ προσορμίζονται,
      ὡς εἰς εὔδιον κόλπον,   **πάλιν εἰς τὸν παράδεισον.**»

ΙΖ

«Ὄμοσον οὖν, τύραννε,   λοιπὸν μηδένα σταυρῶσαι.
      Στῆσον καὶ σύ, Τάρταρε,   βουλὴν μηδένα νεκρῶσαι·
      ἐλάβομεν πεῖραν,   συστείλωμεν χεῖραν·
γένηται ἡμῖν   ὃ ὑπέστημεν
      πρὸς ἐπιστήμην   εἰς τὰ ἐπερχόμενα·
μηδεὶς ἐξ ἡμῶν τοῦ λοιποῦ τυραννήσῃ   κατὰ τοῦ γένους Ἀδὰμ
      ἐσφράγισται γὰρ   τῷ σταυρῷ ὡς θησαυρὸς
      ἔχων ἐν σκεύει φθαρτῷ   μαργαρίτην ἄσυλον,
ὃν ἐπὶ τοῦ σταυροῦ   ἀπεσύλησεν
      εὐφυέστατος λῃστής·   κλέψας καθήλωτο
      καὶ λῃστεύσας ἐκλήθη   **πάλιν εἰς τὸν παράδεισον.**»

ΙΗ

Ὕψιστε καὶ ἔνδοξε   Θεὲ πατέρων καὶ νέων,
      γέγονε τιμὴ ἡμῶν   ἡ ἑκουσία σου ὕβρις·
      ἐν γὰρ τῷ σταυρῷ σου   καυχώμεθα πάντες·
τούτῳ τὰς φρένας   προσηλώσωμεν,
      ἵν' ἐπὶ τούτῳ   ὄργανα κρεμάσωμεν
καὶ ᾄσωμεν σοί, τῷ τῶν ὅλων κυρίῳ,   ἐκ τῶν ᾠδῶν τῆς Σιών.
      Ἡ ναῦς ἐκ Θαρσὶς   ἀπεκόμιζέ ποτε
      τῷ Σολομῶντι χρυσὸν   ἐν καιρῷ, ὡς γέγραπται·
ἡμῖν τὸ ξύλον σου   ἀποδίδωσι
      καθ' ἡμέραν καὶ καιρὸν   πλοῦτον ἀτίμητον·
      τοὺς γὰρ πάντας εἰσάγει   **πάλιν εἰς τὸν παράδεισον.**

thieves, murderers, and publicans and harlots, that they may reap
    sweet fruit from the supposedly arid.
    For they cling to the Cross as to a plant of life,
pressed against it and swimming,
    through it they escape and are brought for anchorage
    as to a fair haven *again to paradise*."

17

"Swear then, tyrant, finally to crucify no one.
    And you, Tartarus, make a firm decision to slay no one.
    We have had our experience, let us draw in our hand.
May what we have undergone become for us
    knowledge for the future.
Let neither of us ever again tyrannize the race of Adam;
    for it has been sealed by the Cross, like a treasure
    containing an unravished pearl in a corruptible vessel,
which a robber, well-suited to his trade,
    ravished on the Cross. For stealing he was nailed up,
    and having thieved he was called *again to paradise*."

18

O most high and glorious, God of fathers and of youths,
    your willing outrage has become our honor.
    For, in your Cross, we may all boast.
To it we have nailed our hearts,
    that on it we may hang our instruments
and sing to you, the Lord of all, from the odes of Zion.[26]
    The ship from Tarshish once upon a time
    brought gold to Solomon, as it is written.[27]
To us your tree gives back,
    every day and moment, wealth beyond price,
    for it brings us all *again to paradise*.

[26]Psalm 136.23.
[27]3 Reigns (1 Kings) 10.21–22.

E

[No title in the Patmos manuscript]

Τῇ δ΄ τῆς ε΄ ἑβδομάδος τῶν νηστειῶν, κοντάκιον
κατανυκτικὸν φέρον ἀκροστιχίδα τήνδε·
προσευχὴ Ῥωμανοῦ
ἦχος πλάγιος δ΄, πρός·
Ὁ χρόνος μου συντελεῖται.

Προοίμιον

Τοῦ φοβεροῦ δικαστοῦ   τὴν ἐξέτασιν
 ἐν τῇ ζωῇ σου, ψυχή,   ἐνθυμήθητι,
καὶ μνήσθητι τῶν στεναγμῶν τοῦ τελώνου,   τῶν ὀδυρμῶν τῆς
 πόρνης,
 κραυγάζουσα ἐν κατανύξει·
«Ταῖς εὐχαῖς τῶν ἁγίων   ἱλασμόν μοι παράσχου,
 ὁ θέλων πάντας τοὺς ἀνθρώπους σωθῆναι.»

Α

Πολλοὶ διὰ μετανοίας
 τῆς παρὰ σοῦ φιλανθρωπίας ἠξιώθησαν·
τελώνην στενάξαντα   καὶ πόρνην δακρύσασαν   ἐδικαίωσας·
 τῇ προθέσει γὰρ προβλέπεις   καὶ παρέχεις τὴν ἄφεσιν·
μεθ᾽ ὧν κἀμὲ ἐπίστρεψον   ὡς ἔχων πλῆθος οἰκτιρμῶν,
 ὁ θέλων πάντας τοὺς ἀνθρώπους σωθῆναι.

5

A Prayer

On Wednesday of the fifth week of Lent,
a kontakion of compunction bearing the following acrostic:
prayer of Romanos.
Plagal fourth mode, according to:
"My time is brought to an end."

PRELUDE

O my soul, during your life,
    ponder the scrutiny of the fearful Judge[1]
and remember the sighings of the publican,[2] the lamentations of
    the harlot,[3]
    crying out in compunction:
"Through the prayers of the saints, grant me forgiveness,
    you who desire all people to be saved."[4]

1

Many through repentance
    were deemed worthy of your love for humankind.
You justified the publican who sighed and the harlot who wept; for
    you foresee their purpose and grant the remission of sins.
With them, bring me back also, as one who has an abundance of
    compassionate feelings, *you who desire all people to be saved.*

[1]Matthew 25.31–46.
[2]Luke 18.13.
[3]Luke 7.44.
[4]1 Timothy 2.4.

Β

Ῥερύπωται ἡ ψυχή μου
  ἐνδεδυμένη τὸν χιτῶνα τῶν πταισμάτων μου·
αὐτὸς δὲ παράσχου μοι   ἀπὸ τῶν ὀμμάτων μου   ῥεῦσαι ὕδατα,
  ἵνα ταύτην καθαρίσω   διὰ τῆς κατανύξεως·
λαμπρὰν στολήν με ἔνδυσον   ἀξίαν τοῦ γάμου σου,
  ὁ θέλων πάντας τοὺς ἀνθρώπους σωθῆναι.

Γ

Ὁ χρόνος μου συντελεῖται,
  ὁ δὲ φρικτός σου θρόνος λοιπὸν εὐτρεπίζεται.
Ὁ βίος παρέρχεται,   ἡ κρίσις ἐκδέχεται   ἀπειλοῦσά μοι
  τοῦ πυρὸς τὴν τιμωρίαν   καὶ τὴν φλόγα τὴν ἄσβεστον·
δακρύων ὄμβρους πέμψον μοι   καὶ σβέσον αὐτῆς τὴν ἰσχύν,
  ὁ θέλων πάντας τοὺς ἀνθρώπους σωθῆναι.

Δ

Συμπάθησον τῇ φωνῇ μου
  ὡς τῷ ἀσώτῳ υἱῷ, πάτερ οὐράνιε·
κἀγὼ γὰρ προσπίπτω σοι   καὶ κράζω ὡς ἔκραξε·   «Πάτερ,
  ἥμαρτον.»
  Μὴ παρώσῃς με, σωτήρ μου,   τὸν ἀνάξιον παῖδά σου,
ἀλλ᾽ εὔφρανον καὶ ἐπ᾽ ἐμοὶ   τοὺς σοὺς ἀγγέλους, ἀγαθέ,
  ὁ θέλων πάντας τοὺς ἀνθρώπους σωθῆναι.

Ε

Ἐμὲ γὰρ υἱόν σου
  καὶ κληρονόμον ἑαυτοῦ ἔδειξας χάριτι·

2

Having been clothed in the cloak of my errors,
  my soul has been defiled.
But grant that rivers flow from my eyes,
  so that I might cleanse my soul through compunction;
clothe me in a radiant garment, which is worthy of your wedding,[5]
  you who desire all people to be saved.

3

My time is brought to an end,
  your awful throne is finally prepared.[6]
Life passes away, judgment awaits, threatening me with the
  punishment of fire and the unquenchable flame;[7]
send me streams of tears and quench the fire's strength,
  you who desire all people to be saved.

4

O heavenly Father, sympathize with my voice
  as with the prodigal son,
for I also fall before you in supplication and cry out as he cried
  out: "Father, I have sinned."[8] My Savior, do not set me, your
  unworthy child, aside,
but gladden your angels as well as me, O good one,
  you who desire all people to be saved.

5

For to me, your son and inheritor,
  you showed your grace.

[5]Matthew 22.11–13.
[6]Matthew 19.28.
[7]Matthew 3.12.
[8]Luke 15.21.

ἐγὼ δὲ προσκρούσας σοι   αἰχμάλωτος γέγονα   καὶ δεδούλωμαι
    τῇ βαρβάρῳ ἁμαρτίᾳ   πεπραμένος ὁ ἄθλιος.
Τὴν σὴν εἰκόνα οἴκτειρον   καὶ ἀνακάλεσαι, σωτήρ,
    ὁ θέλων πάντας τοὺς ἀνθρώπους σωθῆναι.

ΣΤ

Ὑπνοῦντά με ῥαθυμίᾳ
    ὁ πονηρὸς ἐξαγρυπνῶν ἐσυλαγώγησε·
τὸν νοῦν μου ἐπλάνησε,   τὴν φρένα ἐσύλησε   καὶ διήρπασε
    τὸν τῆς χάριτός σου πλοῦτον   ὁ λῃστὴς ὁ ἀρχέκακος·
ἀλλ᾽ ἔγειρον πεσόντα με   καὶ ἀνακάλεσαι, σωτήρ,
    ὁ θέλων πάντας τοὺς ἀνθρώπους σωθῆναι.

Ζ

Χρῄζω τῆς σῆς βοηθείας,
    ὥσπερ ὁ Πέτρος ἐν θαλάσσῃ χειμαζόμενος·
τοῦ βίου τὸ πέλαγος   βαδίζων ποντίζομαι,   καὶ προσπίπτω σοι·
    ἐγγισάτω μοι ἡ χείρ σου   καὶ σωσάτω με, κύριε·
ὡς ἐκ βυθοῦ ἀνάγαγε   ἐκ τοῦ χειμῶνος τῶν κακῶν,
    ὁ θέλων πάντας τοὺς ἀνθρώπους σωθῆναι.

Η

Ἤκουσα καὶ τοῦ προφήτου
    προτρεπομένου με περὶ τῆς σωτηρίας μου·
εἰπὼν γὰρ ἐγγίζειν σε   τοῖς ἐπικαλουμένοις σε,   διεγείρει με
    συνεχέστερον βοᾶν σοι   καὶ καλεῖν σε εἰς ἀντίληψιν.
Τῶν οἰκτιρμῶν σου μνήσθητι   καὶ ἔγειρόν με ὡς Θεός,
    ὁ θέλων πάντας τοὺς ἀνθρώπους σωθῆναι.

But I, the wretched one, striking against you, became a captive and,
   sold to barbarous sin, I have been enslaved.
Have compassion on your image and call me back,
   you who desire all people to be saved.

6

The evil one, keeping watch, made a captive of me who were falling
   asleep from indolence.
The robber, the one who is the author of evil, led my mind astray,
   spoiled my heart and plundered the riches of your grace.
But raise me, the fallen one, up and call me back, O Savior,
   you who desire all people to be saved.

7

I have need of your help,
   just as Peter being tempest-tossed on the sea;[9]
walking on the sea of life, I am thrown into its depths, and I fall
   before you in supplication.
O Lord, let your hand draw near to me and save me;
   as from the depth of the sea, lead me up from the storm of evils,
   you who desire all people to be saved.

8

I also heard the prophet
   exhorting me concerning my salvation,
arousing me to cry out to you more frequently and to call on you
   for help, for he said that you draw near to those who call upon
   you.[10]
Remember your compassionate feelings and, as God, raise me up,
   you who desire all people to be saved.

[9]Matthew 14.30.
[10]Psalm 144.18.

Θ

Ῥύστην σε, σωτήρ, γινώσκω
   μετανοοῦντα ἐπὶ πάσαις ταῖς κακίαις μου·
ἐξάλειψον τὰ πταίσματα,   ὑπόγραψον ἄφεσιν,   ἀμνησίκακε·
   τὸ χειρόγραφόν μου σχίσον   καὶ ἐμὲ ἐλευθέρωσον·
αὐτὸς γὰρ πέλεις, κύριε,   ὁ βασιλεύς μου καὶ Θεός,
   ὁ θέλων πάντας τοὺς ἀνθρώπους σωθῆναι.

Ι

Ὢ ἀφροσύνη· φοβοῦμαι
   καὶ ἐννοῶν τὸν ὀδυρμὸν οὐ σωφρονίζομαι·
πτοοῦμαι τὴν κόλασιν   καὶ ἔργα κολάσεως   διαπράττομαι·
   δειλιῶ μαστιγωθῆναι   καὶ τὸ πταίειν οὐ παύομαι.
Ὀψὲ ποτὲ ἀνάνηψιν   παράσχου μοι, μόνε σωτήρ,
   ὁ θέλων πάντας τοὺς ἀνθρώπους σωθῆναι.

ΙΑ

Μικρὸν ὀδυνᾷ με, οἴμοι,
   ἡ ἁμαρτία δολερὸν ἔχουσα φάρμακον·
αὐτή μοι συνήγορος,   αὐτὴ καὶ κατήγορος   ἀναδείκνυται·
   τὴν δοκοῦσαν συμβουλεύειν   αὐτὴν βλέπω ἐπίβουλον·
αὕτη βοθρίσαι σπεύδει με,   αὐτῆς με λύτρωσαι, σωτήρ,
   ὁ θέλων πάντας τοὺς ἀνθρώπους σωθῆναι.

ΙΒ

Ἀεὶ κρυπτῶς μαστιγοῦμαι·
   τὸ συνειδὸς γὰρ ἑαυτοῦ καταδικάζει με
καὶ κριτήριον κέκτημαι   τὸν ἴδιον ἔλεγχον   τιμωροῦντά με,
   πρὸ τοῦ ἥξω καὶ ὑφέξω   τὸν αἰώνιον βάσανον.

9

O Savior, I know you as deliverer,
    repenting at all my evils;[11]
blot out my errors, O Forgiver, sign the remission of my sins.
    Tear up the record of my debt and set me free;
for you yourself are, O Lord, my king and God,
    you who desire all people to be saved.

10

O folly! I am afraid and,
    considering the lamentation, I do not show sound judgment.
I am terrified of punishment, though I accomplish works of
    punishment. I am afraid of being whipped,
though I do not cease to stumble. O only Savior, late in the day,
    grant me at some time to return to my senses,
    you who desire all people to be saved.

11

Woe is me! So little grieves me.
    Sin, having a deceitful poison,
is shown as my advocate and accuser.
    I see Sin, who is pretending to give counsel, is treacherous;
sin hastens to bury me in a pit. Redeem me from sin,
    O Savior, *you who desire all people to be saved.*

12

I am continually scourged in secret,
    for my own conscience condemns me
and I have as tribunal my own reproach punishing me,
    before I will reach and suffer eternal torment.

---

[11]Prayer of Manasses 7; Joel 2.13.

Ἐνταῦθά με διόρθωσαι   καὶ τότε φεῖσαί με, σωτήρ,
  ὁ θέλων πάντας τοὺς ἀνθρώπους σωθῆναι.

ΙΓ

Νυνὶ καιρὸς μετανοίας
  τοῖς βουλομένοις τὸ τάλαντον πραγματεύσασθαι·
πανήγυρις ἵσταται,   κἀγὼ οὐκ ἐργάζομαι   ἵνα λήψομαι
  τὸν καρπὸν τῆς ἐργασίας   καὶ τοῦ κόπου τὴν ἄνεσιν·
πρὸ τοῦ λυθῇ τὸ θέατρον,   δώρησαι τὴν ἐπιστροφήν,
  ὁ θέλων πάντας τοὺς ἀνθρώπους σωθῆναι.

ΙΔ

Ὁ Παύλου λόγος ὠθεῖ με
  προσκαρτερεῖν σου τῇ εὐχῇ καὶ ἀναμένειν σε.
Θαρρῶν οὖν προσεύχομαι·   σαφῶς γὰρ ἐπίσταμαι   τὰ ἐλέη σου,
  ὅτι πρῶτός μοι προσέρχῃ,   καὶ καλῶ εἰς ἀντίληψιν·
χρονίζεις δὲ ἵνά μοι δῷς   τῆς προσεδρείας τὸν μισθόν,
  ὁ θέλων πάντας τοὺς ἀνθρώπους σωθῆναι.

ΙΕ

Ὑμνεῖν καὶ δοξολογεῖν σε
  ἐν πολιτείᾳ καθαρᾷ δώρησαι πάντοτε·
συμπράττειν τοῖς λόγοις μου   τὰ ἔργα εὐδόκησον,   παντοδύναμε,
  ἵνα ψάλλω καὶ λαμβάνω   παρὰ σοῦ τὰ αἰτήματα·
ἁγνὴν εὐχὴν προσφέρειν σοι   παράσχου μοι, μόνε Χριστέ,
  ὁ θέλων πάντας τοὺς ἀνθρώπους σωθῆναι.

O Savior, set me on the right path here and spare me there,
   you who desire all people to be saved.

13

Now is the season of repentance
   for those who wish to trade in the talent;[12]
the fair has begun, but I do not invest so that I may receive the
   fruit of work and relief from labour.
Before the spectacle is brought to an end, grant conversion,
   you who desire all people to be saved.

14

The word of Paul drives me
   to devote myself to you in prayer and to wait for you.[13]
Having courage, then, I pray; for I know very well your mercies
   and I call for help, that you might first draw near to me.
But you tarry so that you might give me the wages of diligence,
   you who desire all people to be saved.

15

Grant me to sing a hymn to you and to glorify you
   in a pure way of life always;
be well pleased for my words to cooperate with my actions, O
   almighty one,
   so that I may sing requests and receive them from you.
Grant me to offer a holy prayer to you, O only Christ,
   you who desire all people to be saved.

[12]Matthew 25.14–30.
[13]Romans 12.12.

ΣΤ

[No title in the Patmos manuscript]

Τῇ εʹ τῆς εʹ ἑβδομάδος τῶν νηστειῶν, κοντάκιον
κατανυκτικὸν ψαλλόμενον ἡνίκα καὶ ὁ μέγας κανὼν ᾄδεται,
φέρον ἀκροστιχίδα τήνδε·
τοῦ ταπεινοῦ Ῥωμανοῦ αἶνος
ἦχος πλάγιος βʹ

Προοίμιον

Ψυχή μου, ψυχή μου,   ἀνάστα· τί καθεύδεις;
   Τὸ τέλος ἐγγίζει   καὶ μέλλεις θορυβεῖσθαι·
ἀνάνηψον οὖν,   ἵνα φείσηταί σου   Χριστὸς ὁ Θεός,
   ὁ πανταχοῦ παρὼν   καὶ τὰ πάντα πληρῶν.

Α

Τὸ τοῦ Χριστοῦ ἰατρεῖον   βλέπων ἀνεῳγμένον
   καὶ τὴν ἐκ τούτου τῷ Ἀδὰμ   πηγάζουσαν ὑγείαν,
   ἔπαθεν, ἐπλήγη ὁ διάβολος,
καὶ ὡς κινδυνεύων   ὠδύρετο,
   καὶ τοῖς αὐτοῦ φίλοις   ἀνεβόησε·
   «Τί ποιήσω   τῷ υἱῷ τῆς Μαριάμ;
   Κτείνει με ὁ Βηθλεεμίτης,   **ὁ πανταχοῦ παρὼν   καὶ τὰ πάντα**
πληρῶν.

6
On the Infernal Powers

On Thursday of the fifth week of Lent, when the Great
Kanon is also sung, a kontakion of compunction is chanted,
bearing the following acrostic:
a song of praise by the humble Romanos.
Plagal second mode

PRELUDE

O my soul, my soul, wake up—why do you sleep?
    The end draws near and you will be thrown into confusion;
come to your senses then so that Christ God spares you
    he who is everywhere present and filling all things.[1]

1

Seeing the infirmary of Christ opened
    and health streaming from it to Adam,
    the devil suffered, he was stricken,
and being in danger, he was lamenting
    and he cried out to his friends:
    "What shall I do to the Son of Mary?
    The Bethlehemite is killing me, *he who is everywhere present
    and filling all things.*

---

[1]Ephesians 4.10.

Β

Ὁ κόσμος ὅλος ἐπλήσθη   τῶν αὐτοῦ ἰαμάτων,
  κἀγὼ τὰ ἔνδοθεν πονῶ,   καὶ μάλιστα ἀκούων
  ὅτι καὶ δωρεὰν ἰατρεύθησαν.
Ὁ μὲν γὰρ τὴν λέπραν   ἀπέθετο,
  ὁ δὲ καὶ τὰς κόρας   ἐκομίσατο,
  ἄλλος κλίνην   ἐπὶ ὤμοισι λαβὼν
  χορεύει βοῶν· Ἤγειρέ με   ὁ πανταχοῦ παρὼν   καὶ τὰ πάντα
πληρῶν.

Γ

Ὑμεῖς οὖν, φίλοι τῆς ζάλης   καὶ ἐχθροὶ τῆς γαλήνης,
  τί συμβουλεύετέ μοι νῦν   ποιῆσαι τῷ τοιούτῳ;
  Δότε λογισμὸν τῇ διανοίᾳ μου·
καὶ γὰρ συνεχύθην,   ἀπόλωλα,
  οὐδὲν ἐνθυμοῦμαι,   οὐ γὰρ δύναμαι·
  κατεπλάγην,   ἠμαυρώθη μου ὁ νοῦς·
  ἐξαίφνης ἐθάμβησέ με   ὁ πανταχοῦ παρὼν   καὶ τὰ πάντα
πληρῶν.»

Δ

Τοιαῦτα τότε λαλήσας   πρὸς τοὺς αὐτοῦ ὁ πλάνος,
  εὐθὺς ἀκούει παρ' αὐτῶν· «Βελίαρ, μὴ δειλία·
  θάρσησον, κραταίωσον τὰς φρένας σου·
τῶν πρώτων καμάτων   μνημόνευε·
  τὰ ἐν παραδείσῳ   ἀνακαίνισον·
  τοῖς τοῦ Κάϊν   ἐὰν πάλιν κολληθῇς,
  ὡς Ἄβελ ἀνελεῖται δόλῳ   ὁ πανταχοῦ παρὼν   καὶ τὰ πάντα
πληρῶν.

2

"The whole world has been filled with his healings,
 but I, my insides suffer, and especially hearing
 that they have been healed gratis.
For, on the one hand, he put away leprosy,[2]
 on the other hand, he brought back sight.[3]
 Another taking his bed on his shoulders,
 dances crying out: 'He raised me up,[4] *he who is everywhere*
 present and filling all things.'

3

"You then, friends of tribulation, enemies of tranquillity,
 what do you counsel me to do now to this person?
 Give consideration to my purpose,
for indeed I am confounded, I have perished,
 I form no plan, for I have no power,
 I was amazed, my mind was darkened;
 suddenly he astounded me, *he who is everywhere present and*
 filling all things."

4

Then, having said these things to his people,
 the deceiver at once hears from them: "Beliar, do not be afraid,
 be courageous, strengthen your heart,
remember your first labors,
 renew the attack you made in paradise.
 If you again adhere to the people of Cain,
 as Abel was destroyed, he will be destroyed by guile,
 the one who is everywhere present and filling all things."

---

[2]Matthew 8.3; Mark 1.41–42; Luke 5.13.
[3]For example, John 9.1–7.
[4]Matthew 9.6–7; Mark 2.11–12; Luke 5.24–25.

Ε

Ἀκμήν εἰσιν ἐν τῷ κόσμῳ   τῆς σπορᾶς τοῦ φονέως
  καὶ ἱερεῖς καὶ γραμματεῖς, Ἰούδας καὶ Καϊάφας·
  τί ὀλιγωρεῖς ὡς ἀπερίστατος;
Ἡρώδης σου φίλος   διάπυρος·
  Πιλᾶτος δὲ πλέον   θεραπεύει σε·
  τὰς ἀρχαίας ὑπουργίας σου εὑρών,
  μὴ κλαῖε βοῶν· Ἔλυσέ με   ὁ πανταχοῦ παρὼν   καὶ τὰ πάντα
πληρῶν.

ΣΤ

Πολλῶν σου γέμει δραμάτων   πᾶσα ἡ οἰκουμένη·
  εἰς γενεὰν καὶ γενεὰν   λαλεῖται ἡ ἰσχύς σου·
  πῶς οὖν νῦν σαυτὸν ἐταλαιπώρησας;
Οἱ κατακλυσθέντες   ὕδασιν
  οἱ ἐμπρησθέντες   σὲ γνωρίζουσιν·
  ὡς οὖν πάντες ἀπεγεύσαντο τῶν σῶν,
  καὶ οὗτος αὐτῶν ἀπολαύσει   ὁ πανταχοῦ παρὼν   καὶ τὰ πάντα
πληρῶν.»

Ζ

Εὐθὺς δὲ τούτων ἀκούσας   ὁ διάβολος ἥσθη
  καὶ χαίρων ἔφη τοῖς αὐτοῦ· «Εὐφράνθην, ὦ φίλοι,
  ὅτι τοῖς ἐμοῖς με ἐστηρίξατε·
διὸ θαρσαλέως   πορεύομαι
  καὶ τοῖς Ἰουδαίοις   συμβάλλομαι,
  ἵν' ἐκείνους   ἐξαρτήσας τοῖς ἐμοῖς
  διδάξω βοᾶν· ʻΣταυρωθήτωʼ   ὁ πανταχοῦ παρὼν   καὶ τὰ πάντα
πληρῶν.»

5

"The offspring of the murderer are still in the world,
    not only priests and scribes, but also Judas and Caiaphas.
    Why are you faint-hearted as a solitary?
Herod is your ardent friend,
    and Pilate serves you even more ardently.
    Having found your former aids,
    do not weep, crying out: 'He destroyed me, *the one who is*
    everywhere present and filling all things.'

6

"The whole world is full of your many deeds.
    Your strength is spoken of from generation to generation.
    How then have you now suffered distress?
Those who have been inundated by waters,
    those who have been set on fire, they know you.
    Just as all tasted of your deeds,
    so too will he have the benefit of these, *the one who is*
    everywhere present and filling all things."

7

Having heard these things, the devil was immediately pleased
    and, rejoicing, he said to his people: "I am gladdened, O friends,
    for you supported me with my designs,
therefore I march off confidently
    and unite with the Jews,
in order that, having attached them to my purposes,
    I will teach them to cry out: 'Let him be crucified'[5]—*the one*
    who is everywhere present and filling all things."

[5]Matthew 27.23.

Η

Ἰδοὺ δὴ τῶν Ἰουδαίων   τὸ συνέδριον βλέπω
καθ᾽ ἑαυτὸ ἀδολεσχοῦν   καὶ ἀπησχολημένον·
τάχα ἃ λογίζομαι βουλεύονται.
Ἐγγίσας οὖν εἴπω·   Ἀνδρίζεσθε,
ὅτι τὴν βουλήν μου   προλαμβάνετε·
ἐπειδὴ οὖν   σπουδαιότεροί ἐστε,
τί λέγετε νῦν ἵνα πάθῃ   **ὁ πανταχοῦ παρὼν   καὶ τὰ πάντα
πληρῶν;**᾽

Θ

Νὺξ τῇ νυκτὶ ἀναγγέλλει   γνῶσιν ζοφοφόρον·
τῷ Σατανᾷ τὰ ἑαυτῶν   δηλοῦσιν Ἰουδαῖοι
λέγοντες· «Ἀπόθου τὴν φροντίδα σου·
ἃ εἶχες τελέσαι,   ἐτελέσαμεν·
μηδέν σοι μελήσῃ,   ἀμερίμνησον·
παρεδόθη   καὶ ἠρνήθη Ἰησοῦς,
ἐδέθη, ἐδόθη Πιλάτῳ   **ὁ πανταχοῦ παρὼν   καὶ τὰ πάντα
πληρῶν.**

Ι

«Οὐχ ὡς ῥᾳθύμοις προσέχων   ἦλθον, ὦ Ἰουδαῖοι·
καὶ γὰρ γινώσκω τὴν ὑμῶν   σπουδὴν τὴν περὶ ταῦτα·
μέμνημαι τῶν πρώτων ὧν ἐπράξατε,
ὡς μάννα φαγόντες   ἠρνήσασθε
καὶ γάλα πιόντες   ἐψεύσασθε·
οἱ οὖν μόσχον   προτιμήσαντες Θεοῦ,
τί θέλετε ἵνα πάθῃ   **ὁ πανταχοῦ παρὼν   καὶ τὰ πάντα
πληρῶν;»**

8

"Behold, I see the Sanhedrin of the Jews
    discussing and being wholly occupied with it.
    Perhaps they deliberate upon what I plot.
Therefore, drawing near to them, I shall say: 'Be valiant,
    for you anticipate my counsel.
    Therefore, since you are more earnest,
    what will you now say in order that he suffers, *the one who is
    everywhere present and filling all things.*'"

9

Night to night proclaims knowledge,[6] bringing darkness,
    the Jews reveal their designs to Satan,
    saying: "Lay aside your care,
we have accomplished what you are able to accomplish.
    Let nothing worry you, be carefree.
    Jesus has been handed over and denied,
    bound, given to Pilate, *the one who is everywhere present and
    filling all things.*"

10

"O Jews, I came taking heed that you are not being indolent, for
    indeed I know your diligence concerning these matters,
    I have remembered the foremost things that you achieved,
how, having eaten the manna, you denied him,
    and, having drunk the milk, you lied against him.
    You who have honored the calf above God,
    what do you wish that he must suffer, *the one who is everywhere
    present and filling all things?*"

---

[6]Psalm 18.3.

Ι Α

«Ὑπὲρ ὑμῶν τῷ στρατῷ μου   ἐγὼ ἀπολογοῦμαι
    ὅτι ἡμέτεροί ἐστε   ἐξ ὅλης διανοίας·
    μόνον δὲ τῷ στόματι μισεῖτέ με·
καὶ χαίρω ἐν τούτῳ   τῷ σχήματι·
    πολλοὺς γὰρ ἐκ τούτου   συναρπάζετε,
    ἵν’ ἐγὼ μὲν   ἐν τοῖς λόγοις μισηθῶ,
    ἐκεῖνος δὲ καὶ ἐν τοῖς ἔργοις   ὁ πανταχοῦ παρὼν   καὶ τὰ
πάντα πληρῶν.»

Ι Β

«Ῥητὰ τοῦ νόμου Μωσέως   βλέπω ὅτι κρατεῖτε,
    ἀλλὰ μὴ σφίγξητε αὐτὰ   ἐντὸς τῆς διανοίας·
    γλώσσῃ καὶ μὴ γνώμῃ περιφέρετε·
χερσὶ τὰ βιβλία   βαστάζετε,
    φρεσὶ δὲ μηδ’ ὅλως   αὐτῶν θίγετε·
    ἀναγνώστας   καὶ μὴ γνῶστας τῶν γραφῶν
    καλείτω ὑμᾶς καὶ ἡγείσθω   ὁ πανταχοῦ παρὼν   καὶ τὰ πάντα
πληρῶν.»

Ι Γ

Ὡς οὖν ἐστήριξε τούτοις   τοὺς ἀνόμους ὁ πλάνος
    καὶ τὸν θεμέλιον αὐτῶν   ἐνέθηκε τῇ ψάμμῳ,
    ἔδραμε σαλεῦσαι καὶ τὸν Θάνατον·
πρὸς ὃν ἐλθὼν εἶπεν·   «Ἀνάστηθι
    καὶ οἷς ἀπαγγέλλω   ἐπευφράνθητι·
    παρεδόθη   καὶ ἠρνήθη Ἰησοῦς,
    ἐδέθη, ἐδόθη Πιλάτῳ   ὁ πανταχοῦ παρὼν   καὶ τὰ πάντα
πληρῶν.»

11

"I speak in your defense before my army,
    for you are ours with all purpose;
    you only hate me with your mouth,
and I rejoice in this show,
    for you captivate many people thereupon,
    so that while I must be hated in words,
    he must be hated in deeds, *the one who is everywhere present
    and filling all things.*"

12

"I see that you hold fast to the letter of the law of Moses,
    but do not bind fast these things within your mind.
    You carry them about on your tongue and not in your will.
You lift up the books in your hand,
    but you touch them not at all with your heart.
    Let him call you and consider you to be
    readers and not knowers of the Scriptures, *the one who is
    everywhere present and filling all things.*"

13

Therefore, when the deceiver supported the lawless ones with these
    words, and laid their foundation in the sand,[7]
    he rushed to stir up Death also.
Having come to him he said: "Arise
    and delight in the tidings I bring.
    Jesus has been handed over and denied,
    bound, given to Pilate—[Jesus,] *the one who is everywhere
    present and filling all things.*"

[7]Matthew 7.26.

ΙΔ

«Μετὰ πολλῆς ἡδονῆς μοι λέγεις τοῦτο, ὦ δαῖμον·
  ἐγὼ δὲ μόνον εἶδόν σε ὀδύνης ἐνεπλήσθην,
  φόβῳ ἐνθυμούμενος τὰ δεύτερα.
Ὁ γὰρ σιωπήσας ὡς κρίνεται
  φιμῶσαί με ἔχει ἐν τῷ θάπτεσθαι·
  εἰ Πιλάτῳ οὐκ ἐλάλησεν οὐδέν,
  τὰ κάτω σαλεῦσαι σπουδάζει ὁ πανταχοῦ παρὼν καὶ τὰ
  πάντα πληρῶν.»

ΙΕ

Ἀκούσας ταῦτα ὁ δαίμων γέλωτος ἐνεπλήσθη,
  καὶ τῷ Θανάτῳ ὡς δειλῷ ἐμβλέψας ἀπεκρίθη·
  «Ἤδη σε καὶ ἄτονον καὶ ἄθλιον
ἐκ τῶν τοῦ Λαζάρου ἐπίσταμαι
  καὶ ἐκ τῶν ἄλλων πάντων ὧν ἀφῄρησαι,
  ὅτι τρέμεις καὶ τὴν φήμην Ἰησοῦ,
  καὶ δοῦλόν σε ἀχρεῖον ἔχει ὁ πανταχοῦ παρὼν καὶ τὰ πάντα
  πληρῶν.»

ΙΣΤ

«Νῦν ὀνειδίζων με λέγεις ὅπερ λέγεις, ὦ δράκον·
  ἐγὼ δὲ πλέον οἶδά σε φοβούμενον καὶ τρέμω,
  οἶδα καὶ δονούμενον καὶ τρέμοντα.
Οὐκ ἐκ τῶν μνημάτων σὲ ἀπήλασεν;
  Οὐ τῆς Χαναναίας ἀπεδίωξε;
  Μετὰ ταῦτα τοῦ ἀλάλου καὶ κωφοῦ
  ἀλλότριον ἐποίησέ σε ὁ πανταχοῦ παρὼν καὶ τὰ πάντα
  πληρῶν.»

14

"O demon, you say this to me with much pleasure,
  but I, as soon as I saw you, I was filled with pain,
  considering with fear the things that will follow.
For the one who kept silent when being judged,
  he will silence me when he is buried.
  If he said nothing to Pilate,[8]
  he hastens to shake the kingdom below, *the one who is*
  everywhere present and filling all things."

15

When the demon heard this, he was filled with laughter,
  and looking at Death as though at a coward, he answered:
  "I know that since being deprived of Lazarus
and all the others,
  you are not only feeble but also wretched,
  because you tremble even at the report of Jesus,
  and he considers you a worthless slave,[9] *the one who is*
  everywhere present and filling all things."

16

"O dragon, you are reproaching me now with what you say,
  however, I know you are feeling afraid and I tremble,
  I know you are not only feeling agitated but also quivering.
Did he not drive you away from the tombs?[10]
  Did he not chase you away from the Canaanite woman?[11]
  Thereafter, he made you a stranger
  to the mute and the deaf,[12] *the one who is everywhere present*
  and filling all things."

[8]Matthew 27.14; Mark 15.5.
[9]Matthew 25.30; Luke 17.10.
[10]Matthew 8.28; Mark 5.3; Luke 8.27.
[11]Matthew 15.22–28; Mark 7.25–30.
[12]Matthew 9.32–33; Luke 11.14.

ΙΖ

«Οὐκ ἀγνοῶ ὅπερ λέγεις· ἔγνων καὶ παρὰ γνώμην
   ὅτι ἀήττητος Χριστὸς   ἐν φύσει νικωμένῃ·
   ὅμως δὲ τῆς πάλης οὐκ ἀφίσταμαι·
ἠρξάμην γὰρ ἤδη   τοῦ σκάμματος·
   ἐὰν οὖν ἐκφύγω,   καταισχύνομαι.
   Ἀνδριζέσθω   Ἰουδαίων ὁ αὐχὴν
   οἳ πάλαι καὶ νῦν οὐ κατενύγησαν   **ὁ πανταχοῦ παρὼν   καὶ τὰ
πάντα πληρῶν.**»

ΙΗ

«Ὑπάγω οὖν πρὸς ἐκείνους   τοὺς τὰ πάντα τολμῶντας,
   καὶ τὴν αὐθάδειαν αὐτῶν   φορῶν ὡς θωρακεῖον
   τῷ Βηθλεεμίτῃ ἀντιτάσσομαι·
ἀεὶ Βηθλεέμ μοι   ἀντίκειται,
   τὸ γέννημα ταύτης   ἀεὶ βλάπτει με·
   ἐκεῖθεν γὰρ   Δαβὶδ καὶ ὁ ἐκ Δαβὶδ
   ἔφυγε καὶ ἐφυγάδευσέ με   **ὁ πανταχοῦ παρὼν   καὶ τὰ πάντα
πληρῶν.**»

ΙΘ

Ἀπερχομένου δὲ ἤδη   τοῦ πικροῦ πρὸς τοὺς χείρω,
   ἐπῆρεν ἄνω τὴν φωνὴν   ὁ Θάνατος καὶ εἶπε·
   «Βλέπε μοι τί πράττεις, πολυμήχανε·
ἐμοὶ τῷ Θανάτῳ   μὴ πρόσεχε·
   οὐ γὰρ κοινωνῶ σοι   τοῦ τολμήματος·
   ἐὰν νεύσῃ,   προσεγγίζω τῷ σταυρῷ·
εἰ μὴ γὰρ θελήσει, οὐ θνήσκει   **ὁ πανταχοῦ παρὼν   καὶ τὰ πάντα
πληρῶν.**»

17

"I know well indeed what you say; I know also that,
    contrary to what one would expect, Christ was unconquered,
    in a nature that was conquered.
Nevertheless, I do not withdraw from the battle, for I already
    began the contest. Now, if I flee, I am put to shame.
    Let the neck of the Jews be manly,[13]
    they who of old and now did not feel compunction in the face
    of *the one who is everywhere present and filling all things.*"

18

"I go, then, to those who are daring in all things
    and wearing their wilfulness as a breastplate,
    I set myself against the Bethlehemite.
Bethlehem is forever opposed to me,
    her offspring always hurts me,
    for from there David and the descendant of David
    exiled and banished me, *he who is everywhere present and filling
    all things.*"

19

Already while the embittered one departed toward the knaves,
    Death raised up his voice and said:
    "O crafty one, beware what you do to me;
do not give heed to me, to Death;
    for I do not take part with you in your daring act.
    If he beckons, I approach the cross,
    for unless he wishes, he will not die, *the one who is everywhere
    present and filling all things.*"

[13]Cf. Jeremiah 19.15.

Κ

Ἰδὼν δὲ ταῦτα ὁ δράκων,   τοῦ Θανάτου τὸν φόβον,
    τοῖς Ἰουδαίοις προσελθών,   εὑρίσκει ἃ ἐζήτει·
    ἦραν γὰρ αὐτὸν καὶ ἐθεράπευσαν
κραυγάζοντες· «Δεῦρο   καὶ θεώρησον
    τὸν σὲ καὶ τὸν κόσμον   θορυβήσαντα·
    μετὰ ὕβρεις,   μετὰ μάστιγας πολλάς,
    ὡς σάλπιγξ ἐν τῷ ξύλῳ κεῖται   **ὁ πανταχοῦ παρὼν   καὶ τὰ
πάντα πληρῶν.**»

ΚΑ

«Νέον δὲ ἄλλο ἂν μάθῃς,   πλέον ἔχεις γελάσαι·
    εἷς τῶν λῃστῶν τῶν μετ᾽ αὐτοῦ   δικαίως σταυρωθέντων
    κράζει αὐτῷ· ἹΜνήσθητί μου, Κύριε.᾽»
Ἀκούσας δὲ ταῦτα   ἐστύγνασε
    καὶ κάμψας τὴν κάραν   ἐκραύγασεν·
    «Εἰ ἐν ξύλῳ   μαθητὰς χειροτονεῖ,
    ἐν τάφῳ παιδευτὰς καθίσει   **ὁ πανταχοῦ παρὼν   καὶ τὰ πάντα
πληρῶν.**»

ΚΒ

«Οὐκοῦν οὐδὲν ἠδικήθη   Ἰησοῦς ἐκ τοῦ πάθους,
    ἐγὼ δὲ μᾶλλον ἑαυτῷ   ἐπλήθυνα τοὺς γόους·
    Θάνατε, καλῶς μοι οὐ συνήνεσας·
κάλλιον δὲ πράξεις,   ἐὰν φείσῃ μου
    καὶ λάβῃς με κάτω   καὶ παιδεύσῃς με·
    οὐ γὰρ φέρω   τὴν αἰσχύνην τὴν πολλὴν
    ἣν ἔδωκέ μοι ἐκ τοῦ ξύλου   **ὁ πανταχοῦ παρὼν   καὶ τὰ πάντα
πληρῶν.**»

2 0

Having seen these things, the fear of Death, the dragon,
 having drawn near to the Jews, finds that which he seeks;
 for they lifted him up and worshipped him,
crying out: "Come and behold
 the one who troubled you and the world,
 after insults, after many lashes,
 he lies outstretched on the tree like a trumpet, *the one who is*
 everywhere present and filling all things."

2 1

"If you would learn another extraordinary thing, you will be
 able to laugh all the more; one of the robbers who were justly
 crucified with him cries out to him: 'Remember me,
O Lord.'"[14] When the dragon heard these things, he became
 gloomy and turning his head he cried out:
 "Though he is on the tree, he ordains disciples,
in the tomb he will appoint teachers, *the one who is everywhere*
 present and filling all things."

2 2

"Surely then, Jesus has not been injured at all from his passion, but
 instead of him I increased in wailings.
 O Death, rightly you did not agree with me;
but you will do very well, if you spare me
 and receive me into the underworld and educate me.
 For I will not bear this great shame,
 which he brought upon me from the tree, *the one who is*
 everywhere present and filling all things."

[14]Luke 23.42.

ΚΓ

Σωτὴρ ἁπάντων ἀνθρώπων,   μάλιστα πιστευόντων,
    ὅτι βουλῇ ἐσταυρώθης   καὶ γνώμη ἐνεκρώθης
λέγουσι μὴ θέλοντες οἱ ἄνομοι·
ληστῶν τὰ σκέλη   κατεάξαντες,
    τὰ σὰ οὐ κατέαξαν,   ἵνα μάθωσιν
ὅτι ἄκων   οὐκ ἐγένου ἐν νεκροῖς,
ἑκὼν δὲ ἀφῆκες τὸ πνεῦμα,   ὁ πανταχοῦ παρὼν   καὶ τὰ πάντα
πληρῶν.

23

O Savior of all people, especially of those who believe,[15]
    the lawless say unwillingly that you were crucified willingly and
    were put to death of your own inclination.
Having broken the legs of the robbers, they did not break yours,[16]
    in order that they might learn
    that you did not come to be among the dead unwillingly,
    but of your own free will you gave up the spirit,[17] *you who are*
    everywhere present and filling all things.

[15] 1 Timothy 4.10.
[16] John 19.32–33.
[17] Matthew 27.50.

Ζ

Εἰς τὸν Πλούσιον καὶ τὸν Λάζαρον

Τῇ δ′ τῆς ϛ′ ἑβδομάδος τῶν νηστειῶν,
κοντάκιον κατανυκτικὸν εἰς τὸν
πλούσιον καὶ τὸν Λάζαρον, οὗ ἡ ἀκροστιχὶς αὕτη·
ποίημα Ῥωμανοῦ ταπεινοῦ.
ἦχος πλ. β′

Προοίμιον

Εἰ καὶ τῶν ἐμῶν βλέπω πταισμάτων   ὑπὲρ ἀριθμὸν ψάμμου τὸ
    πλῆθος,
    ἀλλὰ τὸ ἄφατον τῶν οἰκτιρμῶν σου
        γινώσκων κραυγάζω· «Οἴκτειρόν με   καὶ **ἐλέησον, Κύριε.**»

Α

Πνευματικῇ ὑμνῳδίᾳ   ὑμνοῦμέν σε, πανάγιε,
    σὺν τῷ ἀνάρχῳ σου Λόγῳ   καὶ τῷ ἁγίῳ πνεύματι·
προσκυνοῦντές σοι ἐν πίστει,
    ὁμολογοῦμεν   τριάδα ἀχώριστόν σε,   τρισάγιε.
Ἀλλ᾽ αὐτὸς τοὺς πίστει βοῶντάς σοι   φωτί σου καταύγασον
    μετὰ τῶν ἁγίων σου,   ὡς τὸν δίκαιον Λάζαρον·
ἀνέγνωμεν γὰρ τούτου τὸν βίον ἐν γραφαῖς
    καὶ τοῦ μισανθρώπου ἀσπλαγχνίαν πρὸς αὐτόν·
    τὸν μὲν γὰρ παρέπεμψας   γεέννῃ πυρός,
        τὸν δὲ κόλποις Ἀβραάμ·   ἀλλ᾽ αὐτὸς ἡμᾶς, οἰκτίρμων,
        τῆς ὀργῆς σου ῥυσάμενος   **ἐλέησον, Κύριε.**

7

On the Rich Man and Lazarus

On Thursday of the sixth week of Lent,
a kontakion of compunction on the
rich man and Lazarus,[1] bearing the following acrostic:
poem of the humble Romanos.
Second plagal mode

PRELUDE

Although I see the multitude of my sins as greater than the number
of grains of sand, yet knowing your compassionate feelings,
which are beyond words, I cry out: "Have compassion on me and
have mercy, O Lord.

1

With spiritual hymnody, we sing a hymn to you, All-Holy One,
together with your Logos who is without beginning,
and the Holy Spirit; we worship you in faith.
We confess you as undivided Trinity, Thrice-Holy One.
As you shined upon the righteous Lazarus, illuminate with your
light those who together with your saints cry out to you in faith.
For we have read in the Scriptures the life of this person and the
misanthrope's heartlessness toward him.
Whereas you consigned one to the fire of Gehenna, the other you
escorted to the bosom of Abraham. But deliver us from your
wrath, O Compassionate One, *have mercy, O Lord.*

[1]Luke 16.19–31.

Β

Ὁ Κύριος ὁ τῆς δόξης,   φιλῶν τὴν ἀνθρωπότητα
    καὶ θέλων πάντας σωθῆναι,   ἐγνώρισε τὰ μέλλοντα,
  προχαράξας ἐν τῇ βίβλῳ
    τὴν ἀπόδοσιν   ἣν δώσει τότε ἀγαθοῖς   καὶ πονηροῖς·
τὸν γὰρ βίον τούτου τοῦ ἅρπαγος   ἀρτίως ἀκούσαντες,
    τὰ ἡμῶν σκοπήσωμεν,   ἑαυτοὺς ἀνακρίνωμεν.
Τοῦτο γάρ φησι καὶ ἡ θεόλεκτος γραφή·
    τὶς ἄνθρωπος ἦν πλούσιος χρήμασι πολλοῖς,
  ὃς ἐνεδιδύσκετο   βύσσον πολλὴν
    καὶ πορφυρίδα λαμπράν,   εὐφραινόμενος ἐν δόξῃ,
    εὐωχούμενος, μὴ βοῶν·   «Ἐλέησον, Κύριε.»

Γ

Ἰδὼν τὸν Λάζαρον τότε   ὁ πλούσιος, ὡς ἄσπλαγχνος,
    ὀργίλῳ ἀπανθρωπίᾳ   τὸν πένητα βδελυττόμενος
  ἀσθενείᾳ τετρωμένον
    καὶ ἀπανθρώπως   ἀποστρεφόμενος αὐτὸν ὁ εὐσθενής,
ὀδυνώμενον δὲ παρέβλεπε   λιμῷ τε φθειρόμενον,
    οὐδέποτε ἐλεῶν   ὁ Θεὸν μὴ φοβούμενος,
ὑπερηφανῶν τὸν ἀδελφὸν ὁ δυσμενής,
    καὶ ἀνηλεῶς βλέπων ἐν πτωχείᾳ αὐτὸν
  γυμνὸν ὄντα πάντοτε
    ἐν τῷ πυλῶνι αὐτοῦ   κατακείμενον ὡς σκεῦος
    τεθλασμένον, κραυγάζοντα·   «Ἐλέησον, Κύριε.»

Δ

Ἡ ὑπερήφανος γνώμη   εἰργάσατο τὸν πλούσιον,
    ἀνελεήμονα φύσει,   ἀπάνθρωπον καὶ ἄφρονα·
  ἐπελπίσας γὰρ τῷ πλούτῳ,
    ἐφυσιοῦτο,   καὶ ἐν τοῖς χρήμασιν αὐτοῦ   ἦν γαυριῶν.

2

The Lord of glory, loving humanity,
 and wishing to save all people, made known things to come,
 delineating them in advance in the Bible,
  he will, at that time, give due fulfilment to the good and to the
  wicked.
Having just heard the life of this rapacious one,
 let us contemplate and examine ourselves closely.
For this is what the inspired Scripture says:
 a certain man who was rich with many goods,
 who clothed himself in very fine linen and a bright purple
  garment, enjoying himself in vainglory, faring sumptuously,
  did not cry out: "*Have mercy, O Lord.*"

3

Seeing Lazarus at that time, the rich man who was vigorous, since
 he was heartless, with an irascible inhumanity, abhorring the
 poor man who was crippled by disease, and inhumanly turning
  away from him,
was overlooking the one feeling pain and perishing from hunger,
 never having mercy, the one who is hostile and does not fear
God, treating the brother disdainfully,
 and unmercifully seeing him in poverty,
 always being naked,
  lying at his gateway like a crushed vessel,
  crying out: "*Have mercy, O Lord.*"

4

The arrogant will made the rich man, who was
 merciless by nature, inhumane and foolish.
 He pinned his hopes on wealth,
  he was puffed up, and he prided himself in his possessions.[2]

[2]Psalm 51.9.

Ἀλλ᾽ ὡς ἔφη ἡμῖν τὸ σύγγραμμα,   λαμπρῶς εὐφραινόμενος,
    τῷ οἴνῳ μεθυσκόμενος,   ἀσελγείαις δεδούλωτο·
ὃς καὶ ἐνδημῶν καὶ ἐκπορευόμενος,
    ἑώρα ἐν γῇ Λάζαρον ψιχίων ἐνδεῆ
    καὶ πρὸ πύλης κείμενον   ἐν στεναγμοῖς,
        τὸ σῶμα βλέπων αὐτοῦ   ἀσθενείᾳ τετρωμένον,
        καὶ οὐδ᾽ οὕτως ἐβόησεν·   «Ἐλέησον Κύριε.»

E

Μακροθυμῶν καρτερίᾳ   ὁ Λάζαρος ὑπέμενεν·
    ὡς δὲ ἑώρα εἰκότως   τὸν πλούσιον ἐσθίοντα,
    ἐπεθύμει καὶ ἐζήτει
        ἐκ τῶν ψιχίων   τῶν ἐκπιπτόντων παρ᾽ αὐτοῦ   μεταλαβεῖν.
Κατακείμενος γὰρ παράλυτος   τραυμάτων πεπλήρωτο·
    δεινῶς δὲ ἐπτώχευεν   ἀσθενείαις κρατούμενος,
βοῶν ἐκτενῶς ἐν τῇ εὐχῇ πρὸς τὸν Θεόν,
    τὰ ἕλκη ὁρῶν τῆς ἀνιάτου συμφορᾶς·
    ὅθεν καὶ συνέπασχον   ὡς ἰατροὶ
        οἱ κύνες τῷ ἀσθενεῖ,   καὶ ἀνέλειχον τὰ ἕλκη
        τοῦ ἐν θλίψει κραυγάζοντος·   «Ἐλέησον Κύριε.»

ΣΤ

Ἀνεξερεύνητα πάντα   τὰ κρίματα τοῦ πλάσαντος·
    τὸν μὲν γὰρ ἐνταῦθα κρίνει,   τὸν δὲ ἐκεῖ εἰς γέενναν·
    ἕκαστος κατὰ τὸ ἔργον
        καθὼς μετρήσει,   καὶ μετρηθήσεται αὐτῷ   παρὰ Θεοῦ.
Ταῦτα δέ τινες ἐλογίσαντο   σκιὰν καὶ ἐνύπνιον,
    ἕως ἂν κατήντησαν   εἰς τὴν γέενναν τὴν ἄσβεστον·
ὡς οὗτος ὁ ἅρπαξ καὶ μισόθεος ἀνὴρ
    τρυφὴν τὰ αὐτοῦ πρὶν ἐλογίσατο κακῶς,

However, as the writing tells us, as he lived in and went forth from
     his home, splendidly enjoying himself, intoxicating himself
with wine, enslaving himself to licentiousness,
     he saw Lazarus upon the ground in need of crumbs
   and lying with sighs before his gate,
     perceiving his body crippled by disease,
     and he did not even cry out thus: "*Have mercy, O Lord.*"

5

Lazarus, forbearing and persevering, abided patiently,
     but, naturally, as he saw the rich man eating,
   he was longing for and seeking
     to partake of the crumbs that were falling from him.
Lying paralyzed, he had been filled with wounds,
     for he was terribly poor, conquered by diseases,
fervently calling out in his prayer to God,
     gazing upon the sores of his incurable misfortune.
   Wherefore, as doctors, the dogs
     suffered with the sickly one and they licked the sores of the one
     crying out in affliction: "*Have mercy, O Lord.*"

6

All the judgments of the Fashioner are unsearchable.[3]
     For while he judges one here, the other he condemns there to
   Gehenna, each according to the person's deeds, as the person
     measures, so will the person be measured by God.[4]
Some people regard these things as shadow and dream, until they
     come down to the unquenchable Gehenna,
just as the rapacious and godless man once considered ill his own
     luxurious living,

[3]Romans 11.33.
[4]Matthew 7.1–3; Luke 6.38.

λέγων· «Οὐκ ἔστι Θεὸς   οὐδὲ κριτὴς
ὁ Κύριος τῶν βροτῶν·   διὰ τοῦτο εὐωχοῦμαι,
ἐντρυφῶ, σκιρτῶ καὶ οὐ βοῶ·   Ἐλέησον Κύριε.»

Z

Ῥύπον εἰ εἶχεν κηλῖδος   ὁ Λάζαρος τοῖς πταίσμασι
   μικρὸν πρὸς ἔτασιν, οὕτω   προσκαίρως ἔνθεν κρίνεται,
  ἕως ὅτου ἀνῃρέθη
      ἡ ἁμαρτία   τοῖς πόνοις τοῦ σώματος νῦν,   ὡς ἐν πυρί.
Οὐδείς ἐστι γὰρ ἀναμάρτητος,   εἰ μὴ μόνος Κύριος·
      ὅθεν ὁ ἐλάχιστος   μετὰ φειδοῦς κριθήσεται,
δυνάσται λαῶν δὲ ἐτασθῶσι δυνατῶς,
      ὡς ἔφη τὸ πρὶν ἐν παροιμίαις Σολομών·
   οὗτοι γὰρ γενήσονται   βρῶμα πυρός
      οἱ ἀμελοῦντες Θεοῦ   καὶ δικαίου ἀποστάντες·
      δι’ ὧν ἡμᾶς ῥυσάμενος   **ἐλέησον, Κύριε.**

H

Ὡς ἐκ πολλῆς ἀσθενείας   ὀχλούμενος ὁ ὅσιος,
      δεχόμενος τὰς ὀδύνας   εἰκότως ταῦτα ἔφησεν·
   «Πρώην μὲν ἐν τοῖς ἀρχαίοις
      Ἰὼβ πτωχεύσας,   ἐγκαρτερῶν ἐν τῇ πληγῇ   ἐρρύσθη αὐτῆς·
ἐγὼ δὲ τὸν θάνατον ἕτοιμον   ὁρῶ ἐναντίον μου·
      διὸ μὴ παρίδῃς με,   ἀλλὰ δέξαι τὸ πνεῦμά μου,
ὅτι κατελείφθην ὑπὸ πάντων ὡς νεκρός·
      ἀπέλθω οὖν νῦν καὶ οὐχ ὑπάρξω λυπηρός,
   κατοικῶν ἐν μνήματι   ὡς οἰκιᾷ,
      ὡς χνοῦς εἰς γῆν κατελθών·   ἀλλὰ ῥῦσαί με ἐξ ᾅδου,
      ὁ Θεός μου, κραυγάζοντα·   **Ἐλέησον Κύριε.»**

saying: "The Lord of mortals is neither God
 nor judge,[5] for this reason I fare sumptuously,
 I revel, I frisk, and I do not cry out: '*Have mercy, O Lord.*'"

7

If Lazarus had a stain of uncleanness because of his errors,
 petty upon examination, thus he is temporarily judged
 on that, until which time the sin is removed
 through the toils of the body now, as in fire.
For no one is sinless, except the Lord alone;
 therefore the least will be judged with consideration,
while the lords of the people will be strongly tested,
 as Solomon said in the proverbs of old.[6]
 For these people who are neglecting God and who have
 withdrawn from the righteous one will become food of fire;
 having delivered us from them, *have mercy, O Lord.*

8

When the holy man was troubled by much disease,
 accepting his pangs, he fittingly said these things:
 "Long ago in times of old
 Job became poor, but remaining firm under the blow,
he was delivered from it, but I see death at hand before me,
 wherefore do not disregard me but receive my spirit,
for I am forsaken by all as a dead person,
 therefore, I am departing now and I will not be sad,[7]
 when I am dwelling in a tomb as in a house,[8]
 as dust descending on the earth. But, my God, deliver me from
 hades as I cry out: "*Have mercy, O Lord.*"

[5]Psalm 13.1.
[6]Wisdom of Solomon 6.6.
[7]Psalm 38.14.
[8]Psalm 48.12.

Θ

Μετὰ τοιαύτας δεήσεις, ὁ πάντα ἐπιστάμενος
    τῷ ἐν ὀδύναις ἐπεῖδεν καὶ ἔπεμψε τὴν λύτρωσιν
δι' ἀγγέλων ταξιάρχων
    τοῦ μεταστῆσαι ἐκ τῶν τοῦ σώματος δεινῶν τὸν εὐσεβῆ.
Τούτῳ δὲ ἀθρόως ἐπέστησαν ὡς φίλοι οἱ ἄγγελοι
    αὐτὸν κολακεύοντες, ὡς δικαίῳ συμπάσχοντες·
οὓς πόθῳ ὁρῶν οὐ θορυβεῖται τῇ ψυχῇ,
    τὴν ἔξοδον δὲ οὐκ ἠγωνία ἐννοῶν.
Τοῦτον ἀσπασάμενοι ὡς προσφιλεῖς
    πορεύονται ἐν χαρᾷ, καταλείψαντες τὸ σῶμα
ἐν τῇ γῇ τοῦ κραυγάζοντος· «Ἐλέησον Κύριε.»

Ι

Ἀλλ' ἀνεθεὶς τῆς ὀδύνης, ἄμωμος ἐπορεύετο
    μετὰ ἁγίων ἀγγέλων ὁ δίκαιος γηθόμενος·
καταφθάσας δὲ τὸ βῆμα
    καὶ προσκυνήσας Κυρίῳ τῷ πάντων κριτῇ, εἶχε χαράν.
Εὐμενῶς δὲ τοῦτον προσέταξεν ὁ πάντα δυνάμενος
    οἰκεῖν [με]τὰ Ἀβραὰμ εἰς τὸν θεῖον παράδεισον.
Μακάριος γὰρ ὃν ἐξελέξω, ἀγαθέ,
    καὶ ὃν προσελάβου ἐν αὐλαῖς σου, λυτρωτά,
κατοικεῖν τὴν ἄφατον δόξαν ἀεὶ
    τοῦ οἴκου σου καὶ ὁρᾶν ἅπερ νοῦς βροτῶν οὐκ ἔγνω·
ἃ καὶ ἡμῖν δωρούμενος ἐλέησον Κύριε.

ΙΑ

Νέμων ὁ κριτὴς ἑκάστῳ τὰ δίκαια ὡς δίκαιος,
    ἀγγέλους ἐξαποστέλλει ὀξεῖς καὶ ὀλοθρεύοντας
συλλαβέσθαι ἀποτόμως
    τὸν μὴ θελήσαντα συμπάσχειν τῷ πτωχῷ ὡς γηγενεῖ.

9

After these supplications, he who perceives all things
 beheld the one in pangs and sent forth redemption
 through the commanders of the angels
 to translate the pious one from the sufferings of the body.
The angels suddenly came to him as friends
 beguiling him, as ones suffering with a righteous man.
Seeing their longing, he was not disturbed in soul,
 thinking of the departure, he was not agonizing.
 As beloved ones walking in joy
 they embraced him, leaving behind on the earth the body of
 the one who is crying: "*Have mercy, O Lord.*"

10

But the righteous man, being set free of distress, walked
 unblemished, rejoicing with the angels.
 Having arrived at the tribunal and
 having worshipped the Lord who is the judge of all, he felt joy.
Graciously, the one who has power over all commanded him to
 dwell with Abraham in the divine paradise.
Blessed is he whom you have chosen, O Good One,
 and whom you have received in your courts,[9] O Redeemer,
 to dwell forever in ineffable glory
 and to see what the mind of mortals did not know;
 bestowing these also to us, *have mercy, O Lord.*

11

The Judge, apportioning to each person righteous things as the
 Righteous One, sends forth swift and devastating angels to
 apprehend in a brusque manner the one who did not wish to
 suffer with the poor man, as befits one who is earthborn.

[9]Psalm 64.5.

Ἀθρόως δὲ τούτῳ ἐπέστησαν   οἱ ἐπὶ τῆς φάσεως
    ἐν προφυλακῇ νυκτός,   οὓς ἰδὼν ἀπεπλήκτησε·
τῷ βέλει τρωθεὶς τῷ τοῦ ὀλοθρεύοντος,
    ἐδίδου ψυχήν, βρύχων τε καὶ ἀγωνιῶν.
  Φανερῶς γὰρ φθέγγεται   ὁ ψαλμῳδός·
    «Τὰ βέλη τοῦ δυνατοῦ   σὺν τοῖς ἄνθραξιν ὑπάρχει,
    ἀναιροῦντα τοὺς μὴ κράζοντας· **Ἐλέησον Κύριε.**»

ΙΒ

Ὄντως τὰ βέλη Κυρίου   ὀργῇ διαπορεύεται
    ἐπὶ υἱοὺς ἀδικίας·   διὸ καὶ τούτῳ ἔφθασεν
  ἡ ὠδὶν ὡς τικτούσῃ,
    καὶ καταλείπει   τὰ πρὶν ὑπάρξαντα αὐτῷ   ἄλλοις ἄκων.
Πάντες δὲ οἱ φίλοι καὶ ἴδιοι   ἐτήρουν τὸν κείμενον,
    τὸ ἄπληστον μεμφόμενοι·   πρὸς ἀλλήλους δὲ ἔλεγον·
«Οὐχ οὗτός ἐστιν ὁ μὴ φοβούμενος Θεὸν
    καὶ ἄνθρωπον ὅλως μὴ ἐλεήσας ποτέ;»
  Καὶ σπουδαίως θάψαντες   τοῦτον εἰς γῆν,
    μερίζονται τὰ αὐτοῦ   ἃ κατέλιπεν ἀδίκοις
    θησαυροῖς· οὐ γὰρ ἔκραξεν· **Ἐλέησον Κύριε.**»

ΙΓ

Ὕλη πολλῇ τῶν πταισμάτων   κρινόμενος ὁ πλούσιος
    εἰκότως ἐνεθυμήθη· «Πολλὰ μὲν ἡμάρτηκα·
  τίς δὲ ἡ αἰτία ἐστὶν
    ὅτι ἐνταῦθα   νῦν τηγανίζομαι φλογὶ   ἀνηλεῶς;»
Ὅτε ταῦτα ἤκουσεν Κύριος   ὁ πάντα ἐπιστάμενος,
    δεικνύει τῷ πταίσαντι   τὴν αἰτίαν τῆς κρίσεως.
Εἰς ᾅδην γὰρ ὤν, ἐπὶ τὸ ὕψος ἀφορᾷ
    καὶ Λάζαρον βλέπει ἐν τοῖς κόλποις Ἀβραάμ·

But the angels delivering the denunciation appeared to him
    suddenly in the watch of the night; seeing them he was
apoplexed. Having been wounded by the arrow of the destroyer,
    with a death-cry and in agony, he gave up his soul.
  Clearly the Psalmist sings: "The arrows of the powerful one exist
    together with the coals,[10]
    destroying those who do not cry out: '*Have mercy, O Lord.*'"

12

Truly the arrows of the Lord come with wrath
    upon the sons of injustice. Wherefore the pangs of death
  overtook him like a woman who gives birth,[11]
    and, unwillingly, he leaves behind to others possessions
that were hitherto his.[12] All the friends and relatives were watching
    the one lying there, blaming the insatiable one; they said to
one another: "Is this not the one who does not fear God and who
    did not show any mercy to a person at any time?"
  And having buried him with haste in the earth,
    they divided his ill-gotten treasures that he left behind among
    themselves, for he did not cry: "*Have mercy, O Lord.*"

13

The rich man, who was being condemned for the enormity of his
    sins, naturally pondered: "I have sinned greatly.
  What then is the cause
    of my being fried here in the flame now without pity?"
When the Lord who knows all things heard these words, he
    showed to the sinner the cause of the condemnation.
For being in hades, he looks on high and beholds Lazarus in the
    bosom of Abraham; therefore he recognized the one who was

[10]Psalm 119.4.
[11]Psalm 47.7; 1 Thessalonians 5.3.
[12]Psalm 48.11.

ὅθεν καὶ ἐπεγίνωσκε   τὸν πρὶν πτωχὸν
    καὶ ἀλλοιοῦται τηρῶν   ὃν παρέβλεπεν ἐν κόσμῳ
    εὐωχούμενος, μὴ βοῶν·   «Ἐλέησον Κύριε.»

Ι Δ

Τότε θαυμάζων ὁ ἅρπαξ   καθ᾽ ἑαυτὸν ἐφθέγγετο·
    «Οὗτος ὑπάρχει ὁ πρώην   ἐν τοῖς προθύροις κείμενος,
    ὃν ψιχίων οὐκ ἠξίουν;
    Καὶ πόσον φέγγος   καὶ δόξαν ἔχει, ἣν οὐκ εἶδον ἐν τῇ γῇ;
Καὶ τί νῦν βοήσω ἢ σκέψομαι;   Αἰτήσω τὸν Λάζαρον
    ἵνα ῥανίδι μικρᾷ   καταψύξῃ τὴν γλῶσσάν μου;
Αἰσχύνομαι νῦν τοῦτον αἰτῆσαι τὸν πτωχόν,
    ὃν ἔβλεπον πρὶν καὶ τῶν ψιχίων ἐνδεῆ.
    Ἀβραὰμ αἰτοῦμαι οὖν·   Πάτερ, βοῶν,
    ἐλέησον τὸν υἱὸν   καὶ ἀπόστειλον ταχέως
    τὸν βοήσαντα Λάζαρον·   Ἐλέησον Κύριε.᾽»

Ι Ε

Ἀδίκως πρὶν τῷ Λαζάρῳ   ἐνήδρευσα ὡς πένητι·
    ἀνομιῶν ἐνεπλήσθην·   ἀδίκως ἐπορεύθην δὲ
    γαυριῶν ἐπὶ τῷ πλούτῳ·
    ἀλαζὼν ὢν δὲ   ἀπεπλανήθην τῆς ὁδοῦ   τῆς ἀληθοῦς,
καὶ τὸ φῶς ἐμοὶ οὐκ ἐπέλαμψεν,   ὅτι οὐκ ἐπέγνωκα
    ὁδοὺς ὁσιότητος,   παροδεύσας τὸν βίον μου.
Παρῆλθεν ὁ πλοῦτος ὡς ἀράχνη καὶ σκιὰ
    καὶ ὡς ἐξανθῶν χόρτος ἐπὶ δώματος·
    ὡς ναῦς δὲ διέδραμεν   ἐν τῷ βυθῷ,
    ἴχνος οὐκ ἔστιν εὑρεῖν·   ἀνωφέλητον οὖν ἐστι
    τὸ ἐνταῦθα κραυγάζειν με·   Ἐλέησον Κύριε.

once poor and became disturbed, observing the one he had
  overlooked in the world while faring sumptuously, not crying
  out: "*Have mercy, O Lord.*"

14

Then, marvelling, the rapacious one uttered to himself:
  "Is this the one who lay on the forecourt previously, whom I
  did not deem worthy of crumbs? And how great a splendour and
  glory does he have, which I did not see on the earth?
And what now shall I shout or consider? Shall I ask Lazarus to cool
  my tongue with a small drop of water?
I am now ashamed to ask the poor man,
  whom I was seeing before in need of crumbs.
  Therefore, I beg of Abraham: 'Father, I am crying out,
  have mercy on your son and quickly send out Lazarus who
  cried out: *Have mercy, O Lord.*'"

15

"Unjustly I formerly ensnared Lazarus, as he was a poor man;[13]
  I was filled with transgressions, but I conducted myself
  unjustly, priding myself on my wealth.
  For being a boaster, I wandered away from the true road,
and the light did not shine upon me,[14] for I did not recognize
  the ways of holiness, passing through my life.
Wealth passed away like a spider's web and a shadow,[15]
  and like grass losing its bloom on a housetop;[16]
  like a ship that has gone into the deep,
  without a trace to be found.[17] It is therefore useless
  for me here to cry out: '*Have mercy, O Lord.*'"

[13]Psalm 9.30.
[14]Wisdom of Solomon 5.6.
[15]Job 27.18.
[16]Psalm 128.6.
[17]Wisdom of Solomon 5.10.

ΙΣΤ

Πλοῦτος καὶ βίος παρῆλθεν· ὡς ἄχνη ὑπὸ λαίλαπος
   καὶ καπνὸς ὑπὸ ἀνέμου ἐκδιωχθεὶς οὐ φαίνεται,
οὕτως μου τὸ πνεῦμα, ἄφνω
   ἐκπορευθέν, ἐμοῦ διεχέθη ὡς χαῦνος νυνὶ ἀήρ.
Σκιὰ γὰρ ὁ βίος παντὶ θνητῷ· οὐκ ἔστιν ἀνάλυμα
   ἐν τῇ τελευτῇ ἐμοῦ, ὅτι σφόδρα ἡμάρτηκα.
Δικαίων ψυχαὶ ἐν ταῖς χερσὶ δὲ τοῦ Θεοῦ,
   καὶ οὐκ ἐγγιεῖ μάστιξ σκηνώματι αὐτῶν·
    διὸ νῦν κεκράξομαι πρὸς Ἀβραὰμ
     ἐξιλεῶσαι Θεὸν καὶ πεμφθῆναι τὸν γνωστόν μου
     τὸν βοήσαντα Λάζαρον· **Ἐλέησον Κύριε.**»

ΙΖ

Εὐθὺς νευροῦται ἐν τούτοις ὁ πλούσιος κρινόμενος,
   καὶ Ἀβραὰμ ἐδυσώπει δακρύων καὶ βοῶν αὐτῷ·
   «Πάτερ Ἀβραάμ, οἰκτείρας
    σπλαγχνίσθητί μοι καὶ πέμψον Λάζαρον δροσίσαι με σπουδῇ.
Τῇ φλογὶ δεινῶς ὀδυνώμενος ἀποτηγανίζομαι·
   διὸ μὴ παρίδῃς με, ἀλλὰ πρόσχες τῇ κρίσει μου·
ἐλθέτω πρός με ὅνπερ παρέβλεπον μισῶν,
   ὁρῶν ἐνδεῆ καὶ ἐκτηκόμενον λιμῷ·
    νῦν γὰρ οὗτος πλούσιος, ἐγὼ πτωχός,
     κρινόμενος ἐν φλογί· διὸ οὗτός μου δροσίσῃ
     χείλη τὰ μὴ βοήσαντα· **Ἐλέησον Κύριε.**»

16

"Wealth and life passed away, just as dust chased away by a tempest
    and smoke banished by a wind are not visible,[18]
  thus my spirit, having suddenly been sent out, is dispersed from
    me at this moment like thin air.[19]
For the life of every mortal is a shadow; there is no liberation in
    my death,[20] for I have sinned exceedingly.
But the souls of the righteous are in the hands of God,
    and a scourge will not draw near their body.[21]
  Wherefore I now cry out to Abraham
    to propitiate God and to send me the one I know,
    Lazarus who cried out: '*Have mercy, O Lord.*'"

17

At once the rich man, though being condemned, is emboldened by
    these words and he importunes Abraham with tears
  and cries out to him: "Father Abraham, feel pity, have
    compassion on me and send Lazarus to besprinkle me in haste.
Suffering terrible torment, I am broiling in the flame. Wherefore,
    do not overlook me, but give heed to my condemnation;
let him come to me whom I overlooked with hate, seeing him in
    need and wasting away in hunger.
  For now, this man is rich, I am poor,
    condemned to flame. Wherefore, let this man moisten my lips,
    which did not cry out: '*Have mercy, O Lord.*'"

---

[18]Wisdom of Solomon 5.14.
[19]Wisdom of Solomon 2.3.
[20]Wisdom of Solomon 2.1.
[21]Wisdom of Solomon 3.1.

ΙΗ

«Ἰδοὺ πατέρα φωνεῖς με,   μὴ γνούς μου τὸ φιλόξενον·
   οὐκ ἂν γὰρ βλέπων παρεῖδες   τὸν ἐν πτωχείᾳ Λάζαρον·
οὗτος γὰρ ὅνπερ καλέεις
   παρακαλεῖται·   σὺ δ᾽ ὀδυνᾶσαι ἐν πυρί,   ἄθλιος ὤν.
Οὐκ ᾠκτείρησας, οὐκ ἠλέησας ἐν τῇ παροικίᾳ σου
   τὸν δίκαιον Λάζαρον   ἐν πτωχείᾳ φερόμενον·
οὐκ ἐνεθυμήθης ὡς θνητὸς τὰ τοῦ Θεοῦ,
   ἀλλ᾽ ἔμεινας μάτην θησαυρίζων τὸν χρυσόν·
   ἐνδεῆ παρέβλεπες   μὴ ἐλεῶν,
   ὡς πλούσιος καὶ φθαρτός·   προστιθέμενος τῷ πλούτῳ
   πλοῦτον ἄλλον, οὐκ ἔκραζες·   Ἐλέησον Κύριε.»

ΙΘ

«Νῦν τῆς προσκαίρου ἀπάτης   ἀπήλαυσα, ὡς ἔφησας,
   καὶ ἐν τῷ ᾅδῃ ὑπάρχω   πικρῶς βασανιζόμενος·
ὅθεν ἐρωτῶ σε, πάτερ,
   ἐξαπόστειλον   τὸν Λάζαρον ὡς ὑετὸν   γλώσσῃ ἐμῇ.»
Ἀβραὰμ δὲ τούτῳ ἀντέφησεν·   «Ἀπέλαβες, ἄνθρωπε,
   ἐν βίῳ τὰ ἀγαθά·   ὅθεν οὐ κεχρεώστησαι·
καὶ Λάζαρος πάντα τὰ κακὰ ἔλαβεν,
   ὡς βέλη τὰ ἕλκη ἐν τῷ σώματι αὐτοῦ·
   ὅθεν οὐκ ἐτάζεται   ὡς πληρωθεὶς
   τῶν ἀπεκεῖθεν κακῶν,   ἵνα τούτων ἀπολαύσῃ
   τῶν καλῶν, ὅτι ἔκραζεν·   Ἐλέησον Κύριε.»

Κ

«Οὐκ ὢν ἀνοικτίρμων νῦν σοι   τοιαῦτα ἔφην, ἄνθρωπε,
   ἀλλ᾽ ὅτι μέγιστον χάος   ὑπάρχει μεταξὺ ἡμῶν,

18

"Behold, you call me father, not perceiving my hospitality;
   otherwise, seeing Lazarus in poverty, you would not have
   overlooked him.
  For this man whom you summon is being comforted; but you,
   being wretched, undergo torment in fire.
During the time of your sojourn, you did not have pity; you did
   not have mercy on the righteous Lazarus
who endured in poverty. As a mortal, you did not ponder the
   things of God, but, hoarding gold,
  you continued to live in vain, not having mercy, you overlooked
   the one in need, since you were rich and perishable; adding to
   wealth further wealth, you were not crying out: '*Have mercy, O
   Lord*.'"

19

"Just now I enjoyed transient deceit, as you said,
   and I belong to hades, being bitterly tortured;
  wherefore I ask you, father,
   send forth Lazarus as rain on my tongue."
But Abraham contradicted him: "O man, you received
   the good things due to you in life, wherefore you do not have
a debt owed to you. And Lazarus received all the evil things, his
   wounds were like arrows piercing his body;
  wherefore he is not afflicted, being filled with evils from there, so
   that he could enjoy these good things,
   for he was crying out: '*Have mercy, O Lord*.'"

20

"I am not being pitiless in saying these things to you now,
   O man, but it is because a great chasm exists between us,

ἵνα μὴ οἱ ἐν τῷ ἅδῃ
    ἐνταῦθα ἔρχωνται, μήθ᾽ ἡμεῖς διαπερῶμεν πρὸς ὑμᾶς.»
Πρὸς ταῦτα τῷ Ἀβραὰμ ἔφησε·   «Σοῦ δέομαι, κύριε,
    ἐγεῖραί με ἐκ νεκρῶν   τοῦ ἀναγγεῖλαι τῷ γένει μου,
μήπως καὶ αὐτοὶ σὺν ἐμοὶ κριθήσονται.»
    Ἀντέφη δ᾽ αὐτῷ· «Ἔχουσι προφήτας καὶ Μωσῆν·
    αὐτῶν ἀκουσάτωσαν   ταῖς διδαχαῖς·
        ὃς δ᾽ ἂν τούτοις μὴ πεισθῇ,   οὐδ᾽ ἐκ τάφου ἂν καθίδῃ
        διανιστάμενον φθέγξηται·   **Ἐλέησον Κύριε.**»

ΚΑ

Υἱὲ Θεοῦ, σῶσον ἡμᾶς   ὡς μόνος ἀτελεύτητος·
    ἀνθρώπου γὰρ αἱ ἡμέραι   ὡς ἄνθος χόρτου ἔσονται·
ὡς χλόη πρωῒ ἀνθήσει,
    τὸ δὲ ἑσπέρας   ἀποπέσει, σκληρυνθῇ   καὶ ξηρανθῇ,
ὅτι πνεῦμα ἦλθεν ἐν ῥισὶν ἡμῶν   καὶ ὡς οὐχ ὑπάρξαντες
    πάλιν γενησόμεθα,   ὡς σκιὰ παρερχόμενοι.
Ἐν τῷ οὖν ἐκλείπειν τὴν ψυχήν μου ἀπ᾽ ἐμοῦ,
    μὴ ὄντος λυτρουμένου μηδὲ σῴζοντος,
    αὐτός με ἐξάρπασον   ὡς λυτρωτὴς
        τῆς ἀπειλῆς τοῦ πυρός,   ἀκατάκριτόν με δείξας
        μετὰ πάντων τῶν δούλων σου·   **ἐλέησον Κύριε.**

lest those in hades
   come here, or we cross over to you."
This being so, he said to Abraham: "I pray to you, lord,
   raise me from the dead to carry back tidings to my family,
lest in any way they too are condemned with me."
   But he answered him: "They have the prophets and Moses;
  let them hear their teachings; but if someone is not persuaded by
   these, not even if he beheld someone rising
   from the grave would he say: '*Have mercy, O Lord.*'"

21

Son of God, as the only everlasting one, save us. For the days of
   man and woman are like the flower of the grass,[22]
 like the first shoot of plants
   it will bloom in the morning, but in the evening it will fall,
harden, and become withered,[23] for breath came into our nostrils,
   and we shall again become as ones not existing,[24]
passing away like a shadow.[25] Therefore, when my soul is departing
   from me and there exists neither
  one to redeem me nor one to save me, as my redeemer, snatch
   me away from the threat of fire, show me uncondemned
   with all your servants: *Have mercy, O Lord.*

[22]Psalm 102.15.
[23]Psalm 89.5–6.
[24]Wisdom of Solomon 2.2.
[25]Psalm 101.12.

POPULAR PATRISTICS SERIES

ST VLADIMIR'S SEMINARY PRESS
1-800-204-2665 • www.svspress.com